An American Renaissance

The Hope of a New Generation

Marcus Johnson

I, Marcus Johnson, do dedicate this book to my family, friends, my wife and children in the future, and fellow Americans.

Prologue

It was not until I reached my teenage years when I learned the greatness of being an American. I did not learn so by reading a book or watching a documentary. America is a place where all things are possible through hard work and determination. It is the dreams and risk-taking of ordinary, everyday individuals for which define America's greatness. Each person is bestowed here on Earth to make a difference for a better world. God has blessed every person with specific talents and abilities, and it is through the fulfillment of a person's abilities and talents that others' lives are affected for the better.

When an entrepreneur takes the risk of starting a new business, tens of hundreds of people will have opportunities for an income to support themselves and their families. They are given the opportunity to climb the ladder of successful achievement; to rise from employee to president and CEO of the entire company. It is not the point of success that makes someone an American, but instead the opportunity to fulfill success. Through realizing that I have the freedom and opportunity to rise to whatever heights as I wish through my own abilities, I learned the underlying greatness of being an American. It was in realizing I could be whatever I aspire to be as long as I am willing to do what I must to.

To be American is just about the single greatest thing a man or woman could be. I do not believe in the myth that a person is limited by skin color or circumstances; every one of us can rise beyond the stars in the sky. I love this country with every piece of my heart, and feel nothing but the greatest for the possibilities of what we as Americans are capable of accomplishing. In spite of the current challenges we face, the United States remains the greatest beacon of hope and prosperity that history will ever record. We continue to provide a ladder of opportunity for our people here at home, extend the arms of justice and freedom to many across the globe, and shed light in the midst of darkness. The world has always been a greater place due to the United States.

You and I know very well that many challenges lie before us; we know beyond a shadow of a doubt what those challenges consist of. Our economy is in crisis, millions of Americans cannot afford adequate healthcare, our education system requires great reform, millions suffer from poverty, and our nation's debt is as high as it has ever been in history. There remains a moral crisis in our country, as well as a problem of gun violence throughout major cities that plagues the lives of millions of children and young adults. We face a very dangerous calamity overseas that demands bold, strategic action. Another great challenge America faces is a profound deficiency of leadership on Capitol Hill.

In the title of this book is the word renaissance; a word we associate normally with the Renaissance Period during the Middle Ages. It was a time that saw the explosion of the arts and literature throughout central Europe, which shed new light to the lives and culture of the people in the area. New ideas and talent rose to great heights and brought new meaning to life. The word renaissance itself is defined as rebirth. Due to the rising challenges we face here in America, so many wonderful-hearted Americans across the land have lost hope in what our destiny holds in store. Many Americans have come to expect the worse for the future and decided to settle for less. It is heartbreaking to me when people regard the direction of our country with hopelessness and despair. More Americans disapprove of our elected officials now more than ever before.

While many of us feel cynicism and doubt for what will become of us, I stand as confident and optimistic as ever. I have strong faith in what America can accomplish because history has shown it time and time again. We have overcome great obstacles in the past, and, as a result, our power has become mightier than ever. I will never fail to recall the 80s when our nation had reached an era of prosperity and promise like no other. President Reagan's bold and patriotic leadership led the United States from the deepest crisis in fifty years to incredible hope and opportunity. He restrained the power of big government and reignited the energy of everyday men and women. He returned them control of their own destiny once more.

We find ourselves in a very similar scenario today with a very clear objective, which is to make America that "shining city on a hill" once again by returning to the ideals that has defined her since the birth of our nation. I am very enthusiastic about restoring confidence to the hearts of every American and have laid out a vision of how to do so in this book. The vision I have outlined in this book are predicated upon a set of values that defines my personal life and the type of country I want to leave behind for the next generation:

A) Peace
•	Defeat radical Islamic terrorism
•	Abolish all nuclear weaponry from the face of the Earth
•	Face our enemies with boldness and clarity of vision
•	Stand with Israel
•	Spread stability and democracy across the globe
B) Togetherness
•	Bridge divisions based upon race, religion, gender, income levels, and sexual orientation
•	Bipartisanship among both parties
•	Respect and honor Americans from all walks of life
•	Exterminate racism, hate, bigotry, and discrimination in all of their forms

C) Hope
- Put our children first
- Offer a positive vision for the future
- Focus on challenges at hand
- Uphold honesty about the issues at stake
- Abandon the loud political noise and refrain from distraction

D) Opportunity
- Encourage entrepreneurship and ingenuity by ending over- burdensome regulations and restrictions
- Initiate tax reform so every American keeps more of his or her hard-earned money
- Give every child a shot at the American Dream by reforming our broken education system
- Eliminate budget deficits, pay down national debt, and establish fiscal stability
- Reform our social safety net by ending incentives of the welfare state and initiate standards and requirements for receiving government aid

E) Freedom
- Return to a limited, accountable, and constitutional government that recognizes and respects the Life, Liberty, and Pursuit of Happiness of every individual
- Remove government from the people's personal and private lives
- Protect and preserve the life of every human unborn child
- Restore the strength and vitality of the American family
- Abolish all laws that discriminates against the LGBT and all other communities

We must remind ourselves that in order to believe in America, we must first believe in ourselves as the American people; for it is we the People who define this great country and her course. Every one of us have the tools and resources in our hearts to make this great, proud, and wonderful nation however we would like it to be.

"The greater the challenge, the more glorious the triumph."

~President Theodore Roosevelt

Chapter 1

Political Awakening

I will never forget the days when I was a small child. At this point in my life, the only things that were relevant consisted of television, toys, and video games. While I cared very much for education and excellence, I did not have a broad and clear understanding of the world and critical issues at stake for the future. I definitely lacked an understanding of the political process and how government works. This is to be expected due to the fact that I was so young in age. Who would expect an elementary school student to understand and yet be interested in politics to a great extent? Certainly no one in this day and age!

I can remember still eleven years ago watching the first of three presidential debates between then-President Bush and then-Senator John Kerry. Previously I was watching my favorite James Bond film Die Another Day until my brother switched the channel to the presidential debate. At this time I was ten years old only. Once again, I held no understanding and interest in the importance of the political process. I went into my parents' room to so I continue watching Die Another Day; however, they were watching the debate also. In my mind, I was doomed to the agony of this boring endurance. In the following two weeks, there an automatic change of heart in regards to the election. Because my family was strongly Democratic and supported then-Senator John Kerry for president, I did so also by instinct. I had no complex understanding still of the issues at hand; the only thing I felt (as a result of family) was the belief that the Democratic Party stands for the poor in contrast to the Republican Party which supports the rich.

It would be a few more years only before my knowledge of public affairs would begin to grow to where it is today. Not only did I realize the importance of knowing what shapes the world we all live in, but the critical role I play in shaping it also. As so much of my perspective has changed, which I will discuss later in the chapter, I have become more inspired to help lead a new generation to greatness. The challenges that lie ahead are enormous and generational. It has become extremely personal for me as I think of my children and grandchildren in the future. It has been long in my heart and soul to build a much safer, better world for them to grow up in; a world where they can have any and all of the desires in their hearts through faith in God and assurance in themselves; where they do not have to fear for their lives as they prepare to sleep at night; where they are accepted and respected by others on the basis of character; and where they can wake up each and every morning with the faith that each day will be better than the last. The worst decision I could have chosen to make was to stand ideally by and accept the failed notion that someone else can do it. I love America far too much and owe it to my children to allow them to inherit the difficulties of today; for this shall not happen on my watch.

Informed and Involved

I am absolute that most Americans hold a very skeptical, pessimistic view on politics, our government, and the future. If you were to ask someone for his or her opinion on the direction of our country, he or she would be most certain to imply that we are headed in the wrong direction. Moreover, if you were to ask someone if our nation is better off than it was five or six years ago, he or she would probably give a very negative or cynical response. As an optimist for the future, I believe that things always improve as time proceeds; but the span of time in which things would improve depends on what we do to bring it about. I feel very strongly that America can meet the challenges that lie before her and fulfill her obligations to the next generation.

I believe with all of my heart that our economy can prosper to the fullest, we can defeat evil in the Twenty-first Century, reform our broken education system, and extend opportunity and freedom to all of those who long for it; for America's best days lie ahead of her. However, none of these things will come about by standing ideally by. Each and every one of us as citizens of this great and wonderful country has a role to fulfill in shaping our destiny. This country belongs to us, the people. It belongs to the students, teachers, entrepreneurs, doctors, and pastors; the sisters, brothers, mothers, fathers, aunts, uncles, grandmothers, and grandfathers; and individuals who are black, white, gay, straight, religious, non-religious, liberal, conservative, rich, and poor. Each one of us are crucial in making America what it is and must be.

We as citizens in this country should be informed well of the challenges we face as a whole and the reality behind them. In holding a deep understanding of the issues at hand, we will know much better how we can and why we must become involved in the political process. The first and most important thing we as Americans should do is strive to learn history. We must know the various ideas and systems of government for which have been met with considerable success as well as those that have failed miserably. Many systems we should be familiar with are capitalism, socialism, communism, and totalitarianism. We should learn, study, and understand the Declaration of Independence and the Constitution. I feel with every fiber of my being that every single American has a moral obligation to know and understand these two important doctrines in their entirety; for they are what guarantee each of us the rights that were bestowed upon us at birth.

Our Founding Fathers were among the greatest human beings who have ever lived, as they were the disciples of their time. They had not only a profound understanding of the world as it was, but a vision for what it could become. They fought a brutal war so their vision could be witnessed and lived by humanity. Men such as George Washington, Benjamin Franklin, Thomas Jefferson, John Adams, and James Madison paid the ultimate sacrifice so we in the present could be free and prosperous. They embarked upon a set of very important principles for which our nation should adhere to.

Today, however, we have a government that has failed to live up to the ideals of our founding; individual liberty, limited government, and the opportunity (not guarantee) for every American to acquire happiness. There are certain individuals who have rejected these ideals deliberately who are serving in high positions of power. As a result, our country has drifted from the vision of our Founders, thus creating the major challenges that plague us today. The reason all of us should know this is so we can know what to search for in candidates for public office. We would be complicit to vote for and support men and women whose world views are based on the idea that government should have greater control over our lives and tell us what we want to hear instead of informing us of the reality of the times we are living in.

When someone tells others what he knows they want to hear, he does not respect them. He does not consider them seriously enough to tell them what they need to hear to better their situation. If my doctor informed me after a physical check-up that I was well and healthy, but in reality I was sick with several diseases, I would not be better off in the long-term. If that were to take place in real life, my doctor could be sued for millions of dollars and terminated of his job. Should not this same criteria be applied to those we entrust to represent us in public office? Should not the institution that is responsible for many of the vital aspects of our lives be held strictly accountable when it oversteps its boundaries? The government belongs to each and every one us as citizens of this country.

The people we elect to serve us possess only as much power as we allow them to possess. When those we elect continue to promise more and more handouts, accompanied with greater deficit spending, we the people must realize the long-term consequences of such actions. We must also never mistake diplomacy and attempts to avoid war for appeasement and diminishing the strength and size of our nation's defense. Our government continues to add trillions of dollars to the national debt; it continues to add millions of Americans to unemployment rolls, destroying their initiative and drive to assume responsibility and do for themselves; it persists to expand its power beyond its constitutional restraints; and it has failed to uphold honesty and integrity. The only way that we will have a government lives up to its obligations is by rising up and taking it back. It will happen by reminding ourselves who we are as an American people. By remembering who we are, we are able to know what qualities to search for in choosing great political leaders.

If you are dissatisfied with the direction our country is headed, you have an obligation to not only yourself but to subsequent generations to make your voice heard on every Election Day. You have a further obligation to encourage your family, friends, and neighbors to vote; it would do none of us any good at all to complain of our present crises with little hope while doing nothing to reverse them. We must terminate the contracts of those who continue to let us down and in turn support candidates who know and understand the principles of our founding based on record. If you stand discontent with the candidates who have been running recent elections, you may want to consider running for public office yourself or encourage someone you know well and trust with your country. We must never forget that America belongs to each one of us and our families and communities. We must take our country back from the special interest groups and lobbyists who have setting our nation's agenda for far too long now. We must reject career politicians who continue to put themselves ahead of the American people. We must proudly remove our government from the hands of the greedy and corrupt and power-hungry and restore character, truth, dignity, and honor to our nation's capital.

You are not required to be part of the intelligentsia; you should not have to be wealthy or well-connected; and you do not have to be a fancy lawyer or corporate executive. It is you; the student in high-student or college; the stay-at-home mom who looks after the children; the father who works at the local plant or factory; the entrepreneur who aspires to be a Fortune 500 CEO; or the teacher who loves your students and will do anything to help them succeed. This is who we are. We have come too far to not change the course of our government. It begins with you and me, the American people.

Change of Heart

I mentioned earlier on that I was a major supporter of the Democratic Party upon developing an interest in politics. At this time, I was an elementary school student only. A few years later, I became a freshman in high-school. It was only a few months before the presidential race between then-Senator Obama and Senator John McCain. I was a strong supporter of then-Senator Obama without a single doubt in my mind. I supported every aspect of his campaign and all of his ideas to restore stability to the country. It was the greatest thing in the world to witness the election of Barack Obama as the first African-American president. I was inspired by his platform of change and making government more accountable to those it is intended to serve.

A committed liberal, I supported ideas such as the re-distribution of wealth, a strong and centralized federal government, and negotiating with terrorists. I was in favor of the choice for a woman to obtain an abortion no matter the circumstances. I was very much sold into the philosophy that individuals belong in groups and government is responsible for establishing an equality of results. I referred to myself as a liberal with no shame; many people I know could witness to this. I would engage in many heated debates with those who disagreed with liberal ideas.

As the year 2009 and the vast majority of 2010 carried out, I would remain a passionate liberal who supported the Obama Administration tooth and nail. During the very end of 2010, my world view began to shift to the Right. In my previous book Believe in Faith: The Power of Christ in You I explained in great detail of the spiritual uprising that had taken place in my life during the year 2010. This was one of the most dramatic events that had taken place in my life. It made a difference in my life for the better. My relationship with Jesus Christ became the foundation of my life. Every decision I would make at this point and beyond would be based on my faith in Him. As my faith continued to grow, I would begin to question some of the things I claimed to have believed in so strongly. Many things became even clearer as I listened to speeches and interviews of prominent conservative figures such as former Lieutenant Colonel and Congressman Allen West, Senator Marco Rubio, and President Ronald Reagan.

My philosophical transformation was rather gradual and challenging than sharp and simple. I realized first that each individual should ensure his or her faith in God as a means to live greatly and achieve success. During the beginning of 2011, I became strongly pro-life on the strength that God has a wonderful divine plan for each individual's life and that no one possessed the right to step in between an individual and the plan God has in store for his or her life. I realized, as a result, that life begins not only at conception but prior to it. God knows an individual and every aspect of his or her life prior to conception. I began to understand that our society is in a moral and spiritual crisis attributed to both the absence of God and the breakdown of families and communities. I became very disturbed by the increasing rates of out-of-wedlock births, teenage drug and alcohol use, and the promotion of sexual recklessness.

I was aware unequivocally by this time that there was a definite war between good and evil. What angered me the most was the Left's deliberate strategy to abolish God from the center of American society by infringing upon our First Amendment, which protects our rights of speech and religion. The First Amendment states the following clearly: "Congress shall make no law promoting an establishment of religion or prohibiting the practice thereof." While government must not promote the worship of God, it also must not discourage it. It is clear that I have become very conservative and spiritual as it pertains to many of the social issues.

As for same-sex marriage and equal privileges for the LGBT community, my support has remained consistently strong. I have yet to witness any major threats imposed on society by acknowledging the God-given natural rights of gays and lesbians. It does not impose any threats to the family or the larger country to establish equal treatment for the LGBT community in the eyes of the law. While my faith says that homosexuality is wrong, it does not permit me or others to judge or discriminate against individuals who are homosexual. Individuals who consist of the LGBT community are just as human and American as the rest of us and should be regarded with the same respect and dignity. I am promoting the behavior of homosexuality itself by no means, but I believe with all of my heart that we are obligated to love and accept everyone as Christ would Himself.

As time would proceed, I began to come around as it pertains to the economy, tax rates, government's role in our lives, affirmative action, and our national security. I realized that people prosper the most when government has a very minimal, limited role. An entrepreneur knows better how to run and operate his or her business in contrast to bureaucrats thousands of miles away who has yet to do so themselves. I began to support the proven truth that people are better off with more of their hard earned money versus the government taking half or most of it. Each person should be recognized with the ability to rise to great heights from the worst of circumstances. While every single person is not promised to achieve his or her full potential, we should not punish those who will through higher taxes and regulations. The American Dream is based on the idea that anyone can realize his or her God-given destiny through hard work and sacrifice. What further incentives will those hardworking Americans have if their successes are punished?

What incentives would others possess if they can receive a handout for doing nothing instead of being empowered to build a legacy of self-determination and successful achievement? The best way to assist those Americans who are struggling to get ahead is to reform our national safety net, which has become a hammock, and provide greater ladders of opportunity through reforming education as well as the tax code and providing greater economic incentives. It is also through realizing that a strong American family play a fundamental role in our economic success. When children are raised with little or no motivation to do great in life, they are likely to enter into poverty, become dependable on government, break the law, and go to prison. I will discuss later throughout the book things we must do to restore the full strength of our economy and establish an environment of long-term upward mobility for those who have less.

The issue for which I have struggled with the most is affirmative action. Formerly I was in favor of it firmly, even as my broad vision shifted to the Right. The more research I did, the more difficult it became in reaching a final conclusion. What disturbed me the most, however, was the fact that an individual could be accepted or rejected for a job or admission to a prestigious university or college on the sole basis of skin color versus ability and merit. As I struggled with this reality, I continued to support affirmative action because I informed myself again and again that someone such as myself would always have the favor. As time carried on, I asked myself continuously if this is not only right and just but truly best for everyone as a whole. After many months of prayer, soul-searching, and further research, I denounced my support for affirmative action. I reached the final conclusion that the long-term method for preventing and eradicating injustice and discrimination is not by re-applying the two methods in reverse. Everyone should be treated with respect and dignity with no regards to race, skin color, religion, gender, sexual orientation, or national origin.

If the goal of affirmative action is to reverse the grave injustices of the past, why does it seek to do so by creating injustices in the present? How would discriminating against hardworking, talented individuals, who had nothing to do with what had taken place fifty or more years ago, lead to justice and equality for everyone? Most of us can agree that an individual should be accepted into a university or chosen for a job on the sole basis of ability and skill. This will not be the case in every situation, however. There will always be some levels of injustice in the world we all live in. It exists among people from all kinds and every walk of life. No government will ever be able to end it in its entirety; however, when racial discrimination becomes institutionalized by the state, more people become at risk. If an employer turns down someone as myself for a job opportunity due to race or skin color, it will be up to me to realize it is not the end of the road.

The first thing I would have to do is re-ensure my faith in God, not man. Then I will be strengthened to search and strive for a job even better than the one I was turned down for in the beginning. I would remind myself that I can achieve much more in life through self-discipline and with the best possible education. After re-applying all of these truths in my mind, I would be reminded of the fact that I am the one who controls my ultimate fate; not government nor a prejudice, discriminatory employer. I know in my heart already that this prejudice, discriminatory employer did not respect me as a person. It would be worse even if my own government does not respect me as a human being by assuming that I am weak and, therefore, should be given pity due to the fact I am African-American. What personal thrill would there exist for me to work for someone who is prejudice and racist? Is it worth forcing him or her to hire me or searching for a job where the employer will respect me as an individual?

I respect myself as a human being not because of the color of my skin, but because I was taught that I can achieve all things I desire if I am willing to believe in myself and persevere to the fullest. I came to realize that an individual's circumstances is related not to the color of his or her skin and solving the issue of discrimination is not accelerating it with more of the same. The Left wants individuals as myself to believe and behave as if we are victims; those on the Left believe that people as myself are too uneducated and not fully capable enough to think and do for themselves. This is the underlying reason I no longer identify myself as a liberal and member of the Democratic Party.

I would also denounce the failed strategy of bowing down to our enemies overseas and dismantling the core of our defense. As I continued to study and research our history as well as that of the world, I would become increasingly convinced that the world is a more stable and safer place when the United States is strongest. I learned that world peace and stability began to unravel after America adopted the policy of isolationism after the end of World War I. Imperialism began to grow and expand throughout Asia and Europe; Nazi Germany and fascist Italy were on the rise; Soviet communism was on the move; and the Holocaust began.

All of this led to the loss of countless lives, the loss of trillions of dollars, and the loss of freedom for tens of millions of people. Much of this lasted not very much longer after the United States became involved. Hitler and Mussolini were in power no longer, millions of Jewish lives were spared, and imperial Japan was defeated. A half of century later would mark the death of communism and the ultimate collapse of the Soviet Union. The world saw a time of peace and great prospects for the future. It was due to not only America's resolve, but our ideals of freedom, liberty, and democracy. I realized that the most effective way for combating evil is not through weakness, concession, and intimidation, but strength, courage, and clarity.

The method for defeating radical Islam is not with more of what we have been seeing in Washington, but with a renewed sense of resolve instead. We must defeat the evil of our time by doing that which has been tried and succeeded in the past; by standing up to our enemies. America has always been the most peace-like country in all the nations of the Earth; it is due to our might as well as our ideals and deepest convictions. We can have the most prosperous and booming economy, the greatest system of education, a balanced budget, and the lowest rates of poverty and crime, but all of this will be for naught if we do not take the issue of terrorism seriously and stand firmly to evil in our time.

As you can witness, my philosophy has transformed to a great extent. I was still a registered Democrat, however, during the two-to-three year change. It was not until the fall of 2013 when I would change my party registration to Republican. It was definitely a struggle in breaching away from my former liberal tendencies due to family and fears of rejection from the African-American community; however, I realized I would gain the support of others and more if I stand on my heartfelt convictions and reach into the hearts and souls of many.

As a motivational speaker, I stress to students and individuals everywhere the benefits of hard work, faith in God and self, and building a legacy to pass on to their children and grandchildren. I have reaped the benefits of these ideals in my very own life, and I realize how important they are in promoting a sense of hope in not only the lives of individuals, but for the entire world. I could bring myself no longer to support a platform that is not only contrary to these principles, but penalizes those children later on by depriving their achievements and destroys the incentive and desire to have greater in life. I also could support no longer a party vision that stands in deliberate opposition with my spiritual faith in God, which has defined my life for the past five years.

Labels such as moderate and conservative do not distract me from the larger picture. It is the history of the two parties that is most significant, which I will explore further on. The Republican Party's ideals of personal responsibility, free markets, community initiative, and peace-through-strength line up clearly with the vision I share for a better, more hopeful future. I will defend these principles tooth and nail on behalf of not only my children and grandchildren, but the posterity of us all. I pray that others will do the exact same and greater in forging a new generation of hope and prosperity.

Exposing the Party of Slavery

It was definitely not easy switching from the Democratic Party to the Republican Party. I must admit a sense of stubbornness as one of the obstacles during my switch. The most important thing to point out is that my change of heart was not by choice, but by realizing the truths of history. As I claimed earlier on, it is essential that we as Americans know what brought us to where we are after two-hundred, thirty-nine years. Upon learning what led us to the present, we can figure out the chart to course for the future. In charting a new course for the future, we must know the reality and contrast between our two parties here in America. As we re-explore transformational events and challenges such as slavery, Jim Crow segregation, and racism, we must keep in mind the roles held by both parties.

Did you know that it was the Democratic Party that was behind slavery in America? Democratic lawmakers instituted policies based on segregation and racial discrimination. Segregationists such as Bull Connor, Senator Strom Thurmond, and Governor Orval Faubus were Democrats. Did you know that Bull Connor led the Alabama delegation in a walkout from the 1948 Democratic National Convention when a civil rights plank was included in the national platform? Did you know that Senator Thurmond opposed President Truman's efforts to desegregate the national military? It was Governor Orval Faubus who attempted to keep the nine African-American students from entering Little Rock Central High School. The original NAACP, which was established by Republicans, was fought tooth and nail by Democrats. Those in the KKK who attacked and lynched countless numbers of African-Americans throughout history were indeed members of the Democratic Party. It is a definite fact based on history that the Democratic Party caused great suffering and despair to people of color.

If it were Democrats who were behind slavery and racial degradation in this country, why does over ninety-percent of African-Americans continue to align with the party? As we answer this question, we must recall that each and every person has the right to support which ever party and/or candidate he or she is the most content with. No one should be forced to adapt to any specific way of thinking; as everyone has a mind to think and decide for him- or herself. I feel, however, that some individuals are just misinformed at absolutely no fault of their own. Some are misinformed by others who are misinformed for the very same reason or by some who have lied to them with deliberately negative intentions. Some people lie often to get what they want, even if it will hurt others in the midst.

Poverty has been the fundamental issue in the African-American community for as long as history can ever recall. As a person who comes from a poor family, I know firsthand the emotional as well as mental effects of being forced to settle for less. As a child, I remember having to wait until Christmas time or tax season for the latest game system or newest action figure. Sometimes I had down to only one or two gifts under the tree during Christmas time. Because I was so young, I would be sad somewhat due to the fact that I had yet to learn the meaning of being grateful for what I have already. At an older age even, I carried the frustration still of not having more. It reached the point where I worried if I would ever lead a life with more for myself and my children later on. There are so many others who can relate to this very same frustration.

This frustration began to become exploited in the 1960s by ideas and policies that consisted of the so-called Great Society program. People were given free homes, welfare with no strings attached, and were told their struggles exist because of people of a different skin color. It is a fact, of course, that the problems endured by African-Americans during this time were due greatly to racial injustice; however, Democrats began to exploit the frustration felt by blacks with a power grab, which soon became a power hold. President Johnson presented himself as an ally of the civil rights movement. He proclaimed once, however, "We (Democrats) will have black people voting for us for over a hundred years" as a result of the so-called Great Society policies. He made this horrific statement also: "These Negroes, they're getting pretty uppity these days and that's a problem for us since they've got something now they never had before, the political pull to back up their uppityness. Now we've got to do something about this, we've got to give them a little something, just enough to quiet them down, not enough to make a difference. For if we don't move at all, then their allies will line up against us and there'll be no way of stopping them, we'll lose the filibuster and there'll be no way of putting a brake on all sorts of wild legislation. It'll be Reconstruction all over again." Do you think that a friend or ally would say something of this manner concerning someone he or she cares for truly? Do you believe the party that supported slavery and Jim Crow laws, initiated the KKK, and made every attempt to prevent people of color from getting ahead was a friend of the African-American community? As a result of President Johnson's and the Democrats' policies in the 1960s, many African-Americans replaced a work ethic based on heritage and deep conviction with a dependence on government involvement and interference.

It was not just hope or recognition of the Constitution that led African-Americans out of slavery, but a spirit of perseverance, determination, and togetherness. As many sought to set out into the sunrise of freedom, they trusted one another and believed in not only themselves as individuals, but each other. This same sense of spirit led their offspring through a century more of profound hatred, racism, and violence. It was replaced with a reliance on promises made by government and an ability to "come through" instead of rising above and beyond. Liberal Democrats crushed the spirit for which rooted deep in the hearts and souls of many great individuals. They were unable to kill it through enslavement, discrimination, and violence; in fact, the spirit became stronger through all of this. Instead they did so through dishonest tyranny; they did so through government handouts and class warfare. The fundamental reason the Democratic Party had taken this course was to enslave African-Americans once again in an attempt to fulfill ambitions for power. Once a man's ability to think and do for himself is diminished, he is turned into a slave; once he is convinced that the majority of his failures are caused by others, he is turned into a victim.

Do not mistake me; I am not proclaiming that every single Democrat today believes in slavery or supports racism or segregation. There are many wonderful-hearted Democrats who have denounced these evils as they are and seek to walk in togetherness and peace with others. However, most Democrats in high positions of power do not believe individuals have the ability to take charge of their own destinies. They believe the negatives in someone's life are at the fault of someone else; they have embarked upon this sense of warfare that pits individuals against one another in terms of race, gender, and income; they believe government is the fundamental solution to the ills of humanity, regardless of what they proclaim verbally.

Most Democrats on Capitol Hill profess a belief in responsibility and hard work and personal sovereignty, but their voting records as well as historical significance simply do not live up to their rhetoric. How can one say he or she honors the American Dream but hinders the means for it to be fulfilled? How can one profess before hundreds or thousands a belief in free enterprise and the success of every American but advocates for burdensome regulations and more and higher tax rates? Democrats should stop professing to believe in the potential of every American child until they begin to support school choice and returning more control of education to parents, local communities, and states.

Take the historical reality of the Democratic Party and apply to today's reality. How much different has it become? The question is not about whether or not it is the party of slavery still, but the tactics used to enslave the individual. Instead of controlling a person through chains and shackles, Democrats seek to control through exploitation and promises. They will exploit the situation of a poor person, who is angry and discouraged, by convincing him or her that he or she is poor because of someone who is better off; they will then promise "assistance" to the poor person. In reality, this creates only a cycle of dependency on government that diminishes the willingness to be responsible for self and overcome the obstacles of poverty personally.

Democrats also destroy the incentives of those who have achieved greatness by taking more of what they earn. Earlier on, wealthy individuals were obligated personally to assist those in their communities who struggled and were less fortunate. Because people were neighbors and knew one another as a result, they knew how to help those who were in need in an efficient manner. This is the very principle of community initiative: helping the people around you who have less. If one of my best friends, Larry Martin, were to approach me for the purpose of advice, encouragement, or financial assistance, I would know how to assist him better because we have a history of being there for one another. As a result, he could trust me and vice-versa. What greater good would it do for Larry to approach an associate who he may not know or trust as well? If I needed a favor or were in serious trouble as a kid, I would approach my parents or siblings before anyone else because I know and love them, which enables me to trust them. The only scenario in which I would approach someone for assistance is when I carry personal assurance at heart for him or her. This was the very case for millions of honorable communities up until the Great Depression.

We are taught in text books that the crisis was too widespread to depend on community alone. In some aspects this was true, but this broke the trust people had in each other and replaced it with a trust in government. This trust has grown greater throughout the decades as the Democratic Party has exploited the emotional frustration of many by turning them against those with the ability to help the needy and less fortunate. When those who have more are regarded as an enemy, they are discouraged from the desire to help those with less and will acquire resentment for them over time.

The Democratic Party portrays itself as an ally of the poor and less fortunate. Imagine if all of those who are poor were to become rich and vice-versa at the snap of a finger. Would the Democrats' "kind" proposals of sincerity and humanitarianism remain so bright and wonderful? Would they continue to carry the same support as before? The only Democratic president who did not exploit people's emotions and struggles was President John F. Kennedy. He will always be one of my favorite leaders in all of history. I feel with all of my heart he would have been the absolute best probably if President Kennedy was given the opportunity to serve the remainder of his first term as president as well as a following term. He advocated for across-the-board tax reductions, a balanced budget, and stood up to the Soviet Union with courage and servitude. President John F. Kennedy was beyond the shadow of a doubt the Ronald Reagan of his time during the 1960s. He will always be the Democrat who was Republican at heart.

There is no doubt in my mind that the Democratic Party in general will remain the party of slavery forever, but will many freedom-loving, hardworking, honest Americans continue to support it? Even as they do, they too are just as American and patriotic as everyone else. However, the Democratic Party and its leadership have failed the United States of America. They have misled us time and time again of the reality of the challenges we face and continue to offer more of the identical unsuccessful ideas of the past. Class warfare, higher tax rates, greater state control and dependency, and socialized medicine have all been tried throughout history all across the world and have led millions of people into deeper poverty, despair, and hopelessness. Democrats continue to champion these very same ideas and always will. While some may be very well-intended, they will never fail in living up to their historical truths. They may sound great by word-of-mouth as well as on paper, but are calamitous when carried out in motion.

The Democrats controlled both the Executive Branch and at least one half of Congress for six years; all they had to show for was greater budget deficits, a runaway federal debt, an increase in poverty and crime rates, and a greater number of individuals collecting unemployment rolls. America continues to suffer, furthermore, from an unstable economy, a broken education system, an unbalanced tax code, and unfixed infrastructure. The Democrats controlled both the White House and both houses of Congess from 2009 to 2011. Within these two years, they failed to reform the nation's broken tax system, immigration system, education system, and, most important of all, restore long-term strength to the economy. Instead they shot a healthcare antidote down our throats that nauseated our savings; a state-mandated system that the American people did not and still do not approve of. This is not the change America voted for in 2008, but there will be a clear opportunity for the nation to chart a new course in 2016.

The Democratic Party fears it to the core when people become empowered by the truth of our time, which is people know far better how to do for themselves than government could ever attempt to do for them. When Americans of all kinds become able to think and do for themselves by re-applying that traditional spirit of faith, perseverance, and fortitude, people such as Al Sharpton and Jesse Jackson, the so-called "black leadership", and the Democratic machine in Washington, D.C. will all go square out of business. I am very confident that the American people will stand up for their future, and hope, greatness, and opportunity will be restored for all.

Re-establishing the Party of Lincoln

At some point in our lives, we will realize times can be rather difficult sometimes to walk the path of righteousness, freedom, and peace. There are periods when such ideals are challenged to a great extent by others that stand in direct contrary. It becomes difficult especially when the effort to encourage responsibility and push for liberty is deemed unpopular in Washington, D.C. and the mainstream media. There came a time in my life when I would realize the profound importance in standing for what is right proudly. It makes not only me a stronger person in the long-term, but offers a source of inspiration for others to stand boldly.

There will always be the few who will stand for truth without question; however, there will be many more who require a voice of hope to speak directly to their hearts. They are either too skeptical of the possibilities of change or simply fear the prospects of persecution if they stand up for truth. When times remain constant for so long, the simplest path to choose is to concede. These are times filled with great frustration and anger and emotional anxiety, with little or no hope for better days to come. This profound sense of disillusionment can be applied to every major struggle in history. This was the case during the nearly four century-long course of slavery; as it continued into the Twentieth Century in the forms of segregation and racial hatred.

During the 1850s, many abolitionist groups began to unite in an effort to end slavery. It was within these groups in which the birth of the Republican Party was established as well as the long-needed voice for hope and freedom. Abraham Lincoln, the first Republican president, would be the leader to cry out the voice that brought an end to slavery in the United States. This marked the beginning of the long, embattled journey to promote the freedom and respect for all persons of color. This was the very motive beneath the establishment of the Republican Party. It was a reaffirmation of the vision held by America's Founding Fathers, and light was shed upon the unjust and vulnerable. President Lincoln brought new meaning and life to the principle that every man and woman should be free and in control of his or her own destiny. He reaffirmed that individuals should be independent and free of bondage from others.

The enslaving of a group of individuals due to skin color will be remembered forever as the most horrific chapter in our history by far. It brought about the deepest and greatest pain, heartache, and misery to the hearts of many. It led to one of the most bloody and deadly fought wars in which mankind can ever recall; a war which marked the end of slavery. A new era in America would begin. It was a time when individuals of every kind from all across this great country would begin to rise and stand firm for freedom and equal treatment. President Lincoln and the Republican Party rallied the nation around a very simple vision; yet it was powerful and unique. The idea that no person should be subjugated to the control of government or any other source of man was the foundation of the Republican platform. President Lincoln and Republicans in Congress brought about the Thirteenth Amendment, which outlawed the involuntary servitude of individuals in this country; the Fourteenth Amendment, which ensures citizenship for every person born in this country; and the Fifteenth Amendment, which protects the right and privilege of every American to cast a vote. During the Twentieth Century, it was the Republican Party that stood for the dignity and respect of every African-American against the humiliation and bigoted idiotism of Democrats and their segregationist methods.

There are many people who do not want us to know the true history of Republican contributions to our country. Did you know that individuals such as Frederick Douglass, Harriet Tubman, Sojourner Truth, and Booker T. Washington were all Republican? Did you know that the first African-Americans to be elected to Congress were Republican? It was the Republican Party that made it possible for African-Americans to run for public office in the beginning! It was Booker T. Washington who established the Tuskegee Institute, which was designed to equip African-American men with the skills to be agricultural and build with their hands. Instead of encouraging his students to dwell on circumstance, Mr. Washington taught his students to believe in themselves, take responsibility, and build a legacy for the future.

Republicans had a goal of not only protecting individuals against discrimination and injustice, but teaching them to stand for themselves and spreading opportunity. Republican presidents were more likely than Democrats to appoint accomplished, prestigious African-Americans to prominent administrative positions. President Ford nominated William T. Coleman as the first African-American to be Secretary of Transportation; President George H.W. Bush nominated Clarence Thomas to the Supreme Court; and President George W. Bush appointed Colin Powell as the first African-American to Secretary of State. After Powell's resignation, President Bush appointed Condoleezza Rice to the position, which would make her the first woman and second African-American to serve it. These are only a few examples of African-American appointees by Republican presidents.

All of this, as with earlier history, disproves all notions that the Republican Party in general holds any tenets prejudice or racial hostility towards the African-American community. The party has proven itself well throughout history as a staunch ally of African-Americans. It extends back to the original vision of President Lincoln and the motivation beneath the formation of the party in 1854. We are taught as if our two political parties swapped philosophies as time proceeded. If you were to study and understand history further, you will discover this notion to be inaccurate also.

A slave was owned and controlled by the slave owner; he or she were told when to eat, sleep, work, and what to wear. Slaves were not respected as human beings and were regarded as insignificant and of little value. Consider how their ancestors felt as their arms were shackled and led onto slave ships. Their sense of dignity and manhood were demoralized; they were belonged to themselves no longer but to someone else. Apply this same fact of history to the reality of today. Consider how someone feels after his or her wealth is taxed at nearly forty, fifty, sixty, or seventy percent even. How about the entrepreneur or business owner who is overregulated by government? What about the farmer who has to battle weather and insects, at no fault of his own, against the overreach of government? We must not forget the unborn child who had no choice of whether or not to continue to live. Most importantly of all, we cannot continue to enslave the minds of those who are less fortunate than others by exploiting their emotional frustration with rhetoric and false promises.

The difference between our two parties can be summed up very simply: Republicans believe in the phrase that goes, "Give a man a fish, and you feed for only a day; teach a man to fish, and you will feed him for an entire lifetime." Democrats believe "Give a man a fish, and you will feed him for a day; teach a man to fish, and you will feed him for a lifetime..... give us your vote, and we will feed you for the next one hundred years!"

Republican principles such as lower taxes, free markets, and limited government have a much deeper, greater meaning. Personally and for others, I believe in leading life based on self-assurance, character, hard work, and the fulfillment of dreams where the limit exceeds far beyond the sky. I do not encourage or support anything for which undermines these values; by that same token, I believe strongly in the means that strengthen and encourage them. Individuals are held captive to failure when the shackles of government control and dependency are present. People become captive once their minds are brought into a warfare mentality; this leads to bitterness, anger, and division. When government raises taxes on some to "lift" others, it undermines the opportunity that has been afforded to each person to become as successful as he or she allows him- or herself to be. Some people will begin to believe as if they are obligated to achieve for themselves no longer but rely on others instead. An individual becomes free once he believes in himself and has the power to achieve what he desires in life. He is free once he assumes responsibility for himself and take full control over his life; furthermore, he must accept the consequences of the decisions and actions he pursues.

In a free society, government will not subsidize the counterproductive behavior of individuals. It favors no person or persons more or less than others through forms of special treatment. President Lincoln said himself greatly, "You cannot strengthen the weak by weakening the strong; you cannot lift the wage earner by pulling down the wage payer; you cannot help the poor by destroying the rich; you cannot help men permanently by doing for them what they could and should do for themselves." All Americans must be regarded with fairness and equality. Everyone deserves an equal shot at fulfilling the American Dream; those who fulfill it deserve to enjoy it to the fullest.

Every American is entitled to keep more of what he or she earns, a fair shot at the very best education, to own as much property as he or she wishes, and live as he or she well pleases without fear of penalty as long as no one else is affected in a negative manner. The Republican Party has stood firmly for this vision from the mid-1850s to the current day. When America experienced crisis during the late 1970s into the early 1980s, President Reagan halted the shackles of government and unleashed the will of free men and women. This led us out of the greatest economic recession since the Great Depression at that time and brought prosperity to heights for which America had yet to rise.

It is once again time the ability of free men and women are embraced and strengthened. It is time the principles of constitutional government, individual sovereignty, and free enterprise are re-applied to the crisis from which we suffer. However, the Republican Party faces major obstacles that are both internal and external. There are many who feel as if the party has become far out of touch with the everyday challenges faced by the American people. Both the Democratic Party and mainstream media continues to portray the Republican Party as favoring those who are well off financially, insensitive to the needs and concerns of minorities and impoverished individuals, and intolerant of women. I will admit that I believed this notion before my heart was opened. From within the party itself, Republicans are conflicted between the so-called establishment and the so-called Tea Party conservatives. Each side attacks the other as being too moderate or too conservative. This sounds no different than little children fighting among themselves over toys or which cartoon to watch on television.

It does the party no good in the long-term, especially as Democrats continue to seize every opportunity offered to connect with the American people. Everyone knows very well of the final outcome after Democrats conduct business as usual. They will exploit people's anger and frustration with deceitful rhetoric and arrogant hypocrisy, which distracts us from the original challenges and worsen them. The time is now for Republicans to stand together once again as one party. The party will rise or fall as one, and it will fall eventually if it does not rise to the demands of time. If this takes place, it will matter no longer how conservative or moderate or libertarian the party is. All Republicans believe individuals should have greater freedom over their personal lives; every Republican believes that taxes should be kept low, private citizens are who shape this wonderful country through their talent and drive, capitalism is the greatest engine of prosperity and opportunity in the world, and the world is a safer place when America is strongest. These ideals continue to shape the banner of the Republican Party. There are also Independents and some Democrats in this country who believe in these principles with all of their being.

The Republican Party must stand for its foundation proudly and let the other side as well as the media define it no longer. It must not change its principles to become more like the other party; this will defeat the purpose of the Republican Party's very existence. The party must tell the truth to the American people as it is and inspire the path that will lead the country forward. It must be the party that connects with those experiencing poverty, women, and the issues in their hearts. Republicans must go into the Hispanic and African-American communities, reminding individuals of history and presenting specific, mindful solutions based on the vision of Lincoln; it can be afraid of reaching out to minorities no longer and carrying forward as if the voices and support of Hispanics and African-Americans do not matter. The party must also refrain from attacks based on negativity and offer a clear, hopeful alternative to our challenges. Most importantly, Republicans must stand with each and every person in America as they have done so in the past. The party is obligated to acquire the torch of leadership in the Twenty-first Century and shape the world for a greater tomorrow.

The American people are fed up of a government and politics that puts their interests and concerns on the back burner; they are tired of being jobless and forced to settle for low-paying jobs, they are fed up with an overreaching, intrusive government; they deserve a sense of security and to achieve their dreams, and they require certainty in home ownership. The American people deserve to give their children a better life than they may have. We have done it before and are capable certainly of making it happen once again.

"Be sure you plant your feet in the right place and then stand firm."

~President Abraham Lincoln

Chapter 2

Understanding America's Greatness

I am sure all of us are able to recall the days of our childhood when we would hear so many wonderful things about this great country. We have seen the posters of presidents and historical figures who have shaped America throughout the course of history. As children we have heard great stories about our nation and asked many questions. We witness the elections of new leaders and view the inaugural ceremonies in-person or on television. In elementary school we study American history and politics from a broad perspective; in some states we test our children's knowledge of the Constitution through a state-administered exam. Most of us will still not understand the core of our foundation as it stands truly. It becomes more clear as we reach adulthood and so on.

As a child, I always knew there was something special about being an American and I loved our country dearly as I do today. I will never forget the day in sixth grade when the teacher told the class about communism in China. After learning that government owns and operates all businesses and property and controls nearly every aspect of the people's lives, it made me very grateful to live in a nation where people are in control of their own lives. This was before I developed political aspirations for the future. Even prior to developing such ambitions, I realized that knowing what defines America's greatness extends far beyond politics as well as posters of great leaders and constitution tests.

Anointed Vision

There are many people all over the world, including those within our very own borders, who dislike and disapprove of America and its founding principles. They do not believe in their hearts that America is the single, most wonderful place on Earth. Some of these people have claimed our nation to be hypocritical, as well as the cause for the evils of international distress.

There are some who hold strong hatred for our great country to the point they would love to see it obliterated and banished off the face of humankind. It should be well expected for hatred for the United States to exist in various parts of the globe. I am appalled forever, however, by many of our very own fellow American citizens who share that very same hatred. Many of them complain very greatly of our flaws with no hope for a better future. They continue their harangue of our values as well as our heritage. Little do they know, they reside in the one nation that provides the constitutional privilege to express such hatred for their own land. They are also able to enjoy the very same freedoms and liberties as the rest of us who love America and are not afraid to proclaim so. The time has come to remind every last one of America's naysayers where our country's greatness originates.

Much of the world has lived under tyrannical oppression for century after century since the beginning of human creation. Nations throughout Europe and Asia endured the tyranny of kings and emperors for longer than any of us in America could ever imagine. If someone was not a member of parliament or the clergy or the elite, he or she would be subjugated to unfair treatment by laws and standards that favored a few only. This was the reality in France for subsequent ages; followed by Spain, Germany, Italy, and Russia. Many attempts had been pursued to abolish monarchy and aristocracy and establish liberty and democracy. While most attempts had failed, there was one attempt that did not fail. In fact it would make a difference and shine a light for the entire world to see. The American journey extends back as far as the early 1600s when a group of men and women agreed in their hearts that no tyrannical form of government deserved authority over their lives. The journey began because these men and women sought the ability to worship the God they loved. They traveled hundreds of thousands of miles across an ocean to a new world to build a greater life for themselves and their posterity. A century and a half later, the descendants of these honorable men and women would sacrifice all aspects of their lives to assume full control and responsibility over their lives.

The descendants declared to the British that each one of their rights of Life, Liberty, and the Pursuit of Happiness comes from God, which makes them inalienable to man. The odds stood highly against the colonial army; as the British navy stood as the strongest in the world at the time. Prior to the revolution, the British were undefeated in world history. Our army stood against the British navy with absolutely no chance for victory. This did not surrender our quest for liberty; not just for ourselves but our posterity also. The colonial army, led by General George Washington, brought us to victory in the face of horrendous challenges and opposition. Our Founding Fathers wrote and ratified the Constitution and the Bill of Rights, which would secure the God-given, natural rights of Life, Liberty, and the Pursuit of Happiness for future generations of Americans. Our Founding Fathers knew best in their hearts the kind of nation their descendants (we) in the centuries to come should inherit. Men such as George Washington, Thomas Jefferson, James Madison, and Benjamin Franklin knew America is better off when each person is free and in control of his or her own destiny. They knew also that humanity is both guided and protected by the providence of God. God would be the One to strengthen us over time and heal the injuries inflicted upon us over time.

Our Founders were among the most intelligent group of individuals to have ever walked the face of the Earth. They were not wealthy or professional as many would expect. Instead they were landowners and farmers who loved their God and stood passionately for the dignity and freedom of all men and women. These men put everything they had at risk so that subsequent generations could prosper to the fullest. We in the current generation will never be able to imagine fully the sacrifices they endured. The torch of freedom would be passed from generation to generation, as it continues to this very day. All of us in this country should be grateful eternally for our Founding Fathers as well as the sacrifices they endured to secure the blessings of liberty. We are indeed their descendants; in blood and spirit both. It is accredited to our Founders that we are able to speak and worship as we very well please, own property and firearms, and pursue our personal lives in a way that pleases us individually. None of this is possible in many other regions throughout the world. You cannot live in countries such as Russia, China, or Iran expecting to enjoy the limitless freedoms and privileges recognized here in America.

Government is not the author of the rights we have as human beings; it is the protector. Our inalienable rights of Life, Liberty, and the Pursuit of Happiness are given to us by God directly. No government or any other institution of Man can take them away. They also cannot establish "rights" of their own to "give" to us such as the right to own a home or healthcare. Our natural rights are what allow us to have and accomplish all of the things we need and desire. Life is the precious gift that allows each one of us to breathe and enjoy physical existence on Earth. Liberty allows us to work hard and pursue our desires and decide what path to take our life. The Pursuit of Happiness ensures us the opportunity to pursue success and achievement in our own way. This must never be confused as the promise of happiness as some would want us to believe. This setup by our Founders has made America the greatest, most exceptional society for two hundred, thirty-eight years and counting. Many nations throughout Europe and Asia would declare their freedom eventually, but it took longer and was far more difficult to accomplish. They are also still living under much rule and tyranny from their governments.

Some Americans who despise their own proud nation have some nerve to do so, especially since they are allowed to express such hatred because of our very own Constitution. To feel this way does not make one any less American; it would be un-American to suppress their right to feel this way. For the rest of us who love this nation to the core in spite of her imperfections, let us never forget the many sacrifices endured by our Founding Fathers. Let us stand forever grateful and proud to live in this wonderful country and call ourselves Americans.

A Colorblind Society: The Sovereignty of the Free

Upon the birth of this wonderful nation we all call home, our Founders recognized the sovereignty of every human being. They understood that America is better when each man and woman is in control of his or her own destiny. They knew also that people know how to do for themselves better than government could ever do for them. The Founders understood greatly that it is the people who make this great country what it is through their spirit of hard work, compassion, and acts of kindness. This has always been the reality here in America, and, because it has, generation after generation has prospered and passed on a greater nation to the next.

There are many in this wonderful country of ours, particularly the Left, who tend to lump and divide individuals into hyphenated groups and classes. They separate individuals in regards to race, skin color, income level, gender, and sexual orientation. Many on the Left believe that African-Americans, which should be Americans of African descent, hold a very strong disadvantage over others in this country. The Left believes that poverty and income disparities exist at the fault of those who are wealthy and better well-off than others; those on the Left believe not in equal opportunity but equal results. Many of the liberal race pimps blame whites for a great deal of the issues faced by blacks; they also bring up the issue of race during instances of gun violence. There is also a notion which floats around that states every person should adapt to a certain lifestyle or belief system due to his or her skin color; it states that character is defined by one's skin color and that someone is different from another automatically if the skin color of the two does not match. This ideology stands as a result of wealth envy and class warfare and a deliberate plot to re-visit past battles for which have been fought and won. We must never use race or skin color or a national crisis of any kind as wedges to divide the American people for the sake of political expediency.

During a time of great challenge and struggle for America, the very last thing that is needed is conflict between individuals based on the concepts of race and background. Instead we need to reaffirm the idea of every American as a free man or woman. We need to preserve the idea of no matter how we may look or what our incomes may consist of, all of us are Americans. All of us are grateful citizens of this great and proud land; Americans of every kind face similar challenges and endure comparable hardships and are together in the fight to form a more perfect union. While there are some in America who prefer to throw us in boxes, our Founders recognized the sovereignty of every citizen. What does it mean for every American to be sovereign? It means that each and every man is given control of his or her own destiny. To be sovereign is to assume the freedom to choose what path to travel and the means by which to do so. Because every person has full control over his or her life, he or she is an individual. Each of us as individuals are unique and beautiful in our own separate ways. We were created by God to be set apart from one another in terms of the wonderful gifts He has rewarded to us at birth.

Our skin colors, incomes, religions, genders, and sexual orientations do not define who we are and our destiny. It is our choice of character that defines us as individuals and the many decisions we make throughout our lifetimes. Because we are free to carry out our lives as we well wish, we must accept the responsibility for the possible consequences of the manners in which we choose to pursue our freedom. There is absolutely no such existence of so-called "white privilege"; individuals of every race and skin color experience great difficulty in terms of finances, emotions, and physicality. There are Americans of every kind who are struggling due to poverty, injustice, a failing education system, etc. Many individuals and families suffer from circumstances foreign to those of others in this country. None of this is due to skin shade; it is because it's life! Life has never been and will never be perfect for anyone, but a person of true character makes no excuses, takes no shame, and strives to overcome and rise high. While some of us endure circumstances beyond our control, there are others who create struggles themselves. A person chooses to dabble in drugs, commit acts of violence, break the law, and fail to utilize his or her full potential. To the contrary, an individual chooses to uphold the principles of dignity and self-respect and create prosperity for him- or herself and others. The ability to do so has no barriers to skin color, which should stand absurd to someone who holds any form of basic intelligence.

Someone who is wealthy should not be held accountable for someone who is not. The one who has less can and should choose to have greater through a change in perspective and decision-making methods. If we seek to assist those who are poor truly, we must address their needs as individuals instead of lumping them together in groups based on race and ethnicity. There is no American that is more or less special than another in any aspect. No one should be treated as such and cast into any hyphenated association. This is a total undermine of the ideal that every American was created to be free. There is no poor, middle-class or wealthy; African-American, white, Hispanic, or Asian; and gay or straight. Each and every one of us are equal and free men and women in the eyes of God and should be in the eyes of one another. The only association we as Americans should assemble ourselves with is that of being an American citizen.

Restraining the Power of Government

The greatest obstacle in establishing the birth of the freest nation in history was the abuse of power from the British establishment. King George III felt as if he knew better than the colonists how to plan out their lives. King George III and the British government felt that it was OK to impose arbitrary restrictions and taxes on the goods purchased by colonists. The British threatened with coercion and violence if the colonies refused to abide by the demands. The colonists realized they had come too far to abandon the promise of their ancestors. They not only stood up to the British with strength, but established a safeguard to big, intrusive government for generations to come. This safeguard would protect us from the unconstitutional overreach and involuntary demands of the state.

Many of the rights we so enjoy such as to speak and worship freely and to own firearms were bestowed to us to ensure the protection of our liberty under law. As we are in total control of our lives as individuals, so must we be in control of the government we entrust; for it belongs to each of us. We the People control how big or small it will be and have a moral and sacred obligation to challenge and replace it when it disregards its original purpose. When government expands beyond its constitutional purpose, our dreams and aspirations at heart become at risk. So what is the purpose for the existence of government in our lives? What did the Founders intend as they were drafting the framework for our nation?

The fundamental, underlying objective of our government here in the United States is to protect the God-given natural rights of Life, Liberty, and Pursuit of Happiness of every individual. These rights were given to us from God directly, which means they cannot be taken away. It is these God-given rights that serve as the tools we need to prosper and pass it on to subsequent generations. Our government has never been granted permission to establish new rights such as the right to own a home, the right to free healthcare, and the right to sit at home on our backs while other hardworking Americans are breaking their backs each and every day. When government begins the act of giving out free items and services, it puts us on a very dangerous path to a culture of dependency and entitlement, which is exactly the path we headed down currently. Government must protect our natural rights by fulfilling these three principles:

A) Create the framework for economic successful achievement.
B) Commit to a strong national defense and vibrant foreign policy.
C) Ensure the equal treatment of every American in the eyes of the law with no regards to race, gender, income, religion, and sexual orientation.

The purpose of government is not to make it difficult and impossible to pursue our freedom and fulfill our aspirations, but instead the opposite by doing that which is obvious. Government policies should stand on common sense and aim for what is best in the long-term. It should never act as if it knows better than people to do what they do best. Government should never do for people what they can and should do for themselves such as owning and operating our businesses and raising our children; it also should not hardened the process of either. As President Reagan proclaimed it best, "We the People are the driver of the car, while government sits in the passenger seat. We the People tell it where to go; it (government) does not tell us where to go." History has proven well that nations prosper the most when government does the least. To the contrary, societies have suffered and eventually collapsed when government exceeds its moral boundaries.

The first objective of our government in protecting our Life, Liberty, and Pursuit of Happiness is to underline the foundation for economic successful achievement. What does it mean for government to do this? It means simply to set conditions where the people can have the confidence that their hard work will be rewarded. There is one side that believes government is the fundamental driver of economic growth in America. They believe in the systems of entitlement and the welfare state. They believe also that businesses do best when they are overregulated and overtaxed. We have seen the results of this failed, Marxist ideology not only here in our country but throughout the world. More and more taxes, greater regulations on businesses, and increased government dependency do not reward hard work, but discourage it.

The American Dream has always relied upon the dreams and aspirations of ordinary men and women. It depends on the ability of individuals to pursue success through self-determination and hard work. Every American deserves to achieve as much greatness as he or she wishes as long as he or she is willing to seek and strive for it. Every single American deserves a shot to build a better life for him- or herself and family. Government should not stand in the way of people in doing so; it also should not encourage dependency through a check to do absolutely nothing instead of earning an honest, decent living.

Government must set the framework for growth and success by doing the following: creating a regulatory system that ensures the safety of consumers and workers without stifling productivity; lowering tax rates across the board so that individuals and businesses can keep more of their hard-earned wealth; creating an education system that puts students first by helping them acquire the skills required to master the Twenty-First Century; and returning our nation to fiscal stability. There must also be major reform of America's safety-net to eliminate fraud and abuse as we seek to help those who need it revive themselves. It will be exploited and abused if there are no limits and standards in place. It is just as great of a tyranny with an open hand versus an iron fist. Every single American will not choose the path of success through opportunity, but more will do so if government does not discourage the act of doing so.

The second objective of government must be to protect the American people from those who would inflict harm and terror. This was one of the greatest concerns of our Founding Fathers. America can have the greatest, most productive economy, adequate infrastructure, a great education system, and a safe environment; however, none of it would do us anything good without protection from terrorism. We live in a very dangerous world, and the last thing we can afford is to play around by not preparing ourselves for the worst. We cannot and must not regard the threat of terrorism lightly. We cannot continue to appease the enemy and negotiate with those who wish to annihilate us at any cost. Government has a solemn responsibility to protect us from the underwear bombers and those who would slash the heads and throats of innocent civilians.

Those on the far Left want us to believe that war should never be an option, even in the necessary circumstances. They exploit our fears and emotional concerns instead of being truly honest about the challenges we face and what must be done to keep us safe. A strong military has always been proven good for America and its long-term safety. Every American citizen deserves certainty and peace in the assurance of safety. None of us should be forced to sleep in fear that our children may not live to witness the next light of day. Government must never shrink from the obligations to our men and women in uniform; they must be provided the weaponry and supplies necessary when called to arms. They should also be supported and nurtured when upon arrival back onto shore. The United States of America has the strongest, most powerful military in the entire world. No reason exists under the Sun as to why our government should not fulfill its solemn responsibility of ensuring the safety of every American from danger abroad.

The third and final objective of government in protecting our Life, Liberty, and Pursuit of Happiness is ensuring the equal treatment of Americans under the law of every race, gender, sexual orientation, religion, and gender. This country has long battled the terrible poisons of injustice and discrimination of individuals from every walk of life. Over the past century and a half, we have reaffirmed the promise of liberty through the abolishing of slavery and establishment of civil rights for all as well as the right to vote. As we eye the horizon, we would see large scales of unequal treatment to some individuals. There are many people in America who have yet to overcome the ill of prejudice in all of its forms. Racism, bigotry, and discrimination hurt and destroy the lives of ordinary, everyday men, women, and children. Most of these Americans affected are honest, good-hearted citizens who only seek to live in peace and harmony. I am offended very heavily by the acts of unfair treatment to those who do not deserve it, especially when it extends from the hands of our very own government. It happens because the skin color or gender or lifestyle of a person or persons does not sit well with some. This should not prohibit certain individuals from pursuing and enjoying their God-given rights as citizens of the freest nation on Earth.

Government is obligated to establish and strictly enforce laws that prohibit unfair treatment of any person due to the factors listed above. It should not extend special treatment to individuals due to race, religion, sexual orientation, or gender, but ensure that all Americans share the same privileges and live by the same laws. There is much discrimination that exists in the LGBT community, which I will discuss in greater detail in a much later chapter. This discrimination must end immediately if we are to continue on as a free nation. We must end the act of determining employment and college admission based on race also. It is one thing to be discriminated against by someone you never have to see again, but beyond a moral tragedy when it is your very own government.

Standing Firm in Our Identity

Our sense of identity as an American people is the most unique in human history. Our Constitution was written and ratified over two centuries ago and its fire burns as bright today as it has then. The principles for which sustain our exceptionalism differ from those in places such as Russia and China and Iran. Unlike these countries where there exists many restrictions on personal freedom, we are free to do as we please as long as we do not affect others in a negative manner. While each of us are individuals, we have never failed to bond with those in our neighborhoods, schools, churches, and communities. Capitalism allows us to utilize the full spectrum of our resources and achieve limitless wealth and opportunity. Our republic form of government bestows to us a free and open political process that ensures every voice to be heard, in spite of the loud noise and political correctness.

The Left is seeking deliberately to fundamentally re-define America to something it was not intended by the Founding Fathers. They continuously mistake capitalism and free enterprise as the causes for poverty, homelessness, and "income inequality." They believe America is the cause of evil throughout the world. The Left is seeking also to remove God from the core of our nation's foundation. All of us know the philosophy the Left believes in strongly. Many of our children are being brought up into it and not being taught the truth of our profound greatness as a nation. The Left is pursuing a very dangerous agenda for America's future, amd it will not be long before the pendulum is reached. If we are to remain the greatest nation on Earth, we must remain true to what makes us who we are. We must remain loyal to the principles and ideals that sustain greatness in our lives and extend them to our offspring. Our children deserve a nation where they are recognized as the unique individuals they are rather than a collective group of races and factions. They deserve a nation where they are honored as citizens in a free society and not subjugated to the unrestricted power and overreach of big government.

We are the generation that must choose to stand firm in what we honor as Americans. Our Founding Fathers sacrificed far too much for us to surrender the legacy they passed onto us. Our ancestors fought too hard and shed too much blood for us to escape the responsibility of doing the same for our posterity. We have come much too far as a nation to re-define who we are as Americans and relinquish now from maintaining our greatness. Let us choose to make our future what it must be for our children and grandchildren. After all, they deserve it more than anything else we have to offer.

"Prudence, indeed, will dictate that Governments long established should not be changed for light and transient causes; and accordingly all experience hath shown, that mankind are more disposed to suffer, while evils are sufferable, than to right themselves by abolishing the forms to which they are accustomed. But when a long train of abuses and usurpations, pursuing invariably the same Object evinces a design to reduce them under absolute Despotism, it is their right, it is their duty, to throw off such Government, and to provide new Guards for their future security."

~Thomas Jefferson

Chapter 3

A New Dawn of Leadership

The United States of America has stood as the greatest nation that civilization has known since the dawn of time. We are the most exceptional society in all of the world. America holds more wealth than any other industrialized country on Earth. We have the most prosperous economy, the mightiest defense, and system of government where individuals are free to make their voices heard. Each and every person can accomplish any dream, fulfill any goal, and overcome all obstacles through dedication and personal initiative. People from every corner of life are afforded the same rights and opportunities by the Constitution. While America remains with great imperfection, it has never failed to outperform the world and extend a better life to those who seek it.

I wake up each and every morning grateful to be called an American. I do my very best to never take for granted the chance to pursue life, liberty, and happiness. I will always recognize the fact that I would never be able to live free and prosperously in many other nations as I would here in the United States. No matter what iniquities that may exist, America will never cease to uphold its superiority. There are very critical concerns, however, that must be met: if our country is as great as many say it is, then what is the problem? Why are there so many hard-touching challenges at hand? I will do my absolute best to address these concerns and offer long-term solutions throughout the chapter. Never cease to remember that something wonderful and great can have flaws still, but they should never be used as excuses to escape the issues we must meet head-on.

An American Hero

How would you define a hero? Would you say it is someone who saves the day? How about a person who has saved the life of another human being or animal? Could a hero possibly be the one who prevents something terrible or tragic from taking place? All of these are accepted examples of heroes. My definition of a hero is someone who leaves others in a better position than they were before. I admire many individuals who has done things that have left people better off than before; for example, Jesus Christ, Abraham Lincoln, and Martin Luther King, Jr. One individual who I admire with all of my heart and consider a hero is none other than former president, Ronald Reagan. I feel he is one of the greatest persons who has received the privilege to walk the face of the Earth. There are many things that qualify Mr. Reagan as one of the best men to serve as our nation's leader. President Reagan did much more than reaffirm the health and vitality to a very fragile economy and bring communist totalitarianism to its demise. He restored confidence and hope into the hearts of the American people after years of crisis and failed leadership. President Reagan re-ignited a sense of patriotism for which had been long lost.

Similar to now, America was experiencing its greatest downfall in history during the late 1970s, which sprung into the early 80s. Many intellectuals, both conservative and liberal, predicted the end of our greatness as a nation at home and throughout the world.

They proclaimed again and again that the economy was doomed to failure and the Soviet Union was not only undefeatable, but would surpass the United States as the world's dominant power. It stuns me how these guys were selling out their very own proud country to death. President Carter himself even began to exceed hope for our nation's future. He went even as far as to proclaim it was at the fault of the American people that our country was in the midst of crisis. This embarrassing sense of pessimism began soon to approach the hearts of the American people. It would only worsen as interests rates and inflation continued to rise, more layoffs occurred, oil prices rose higher and higher, and as American hostages were held captive in Iran. It was Ronald Reagan who offered a new vision for the future.

He reminded us of the ideals and principles that defined us as a free society. As a presidential candidate, he made it his all to remind us that the crises existed not at our fault but those we entrusted to lead us. Candidate Reagan reminded us that our trust belongs not in government but in our ability as individuals and communities to shape the world as we saw it fit. As president, he did not use the reckless and failed record of the previous administration as an excuse for the challenges that were at hand. President Reagan assumed full responsibility for the work that needed to be done. Without a shadow of a doubt, he did exactly that. He cut taxes for every American, curbed inflation and interest rates, reduced unnecessary regulations on businesses and industry, and increased the strength our military defense. President Reagan's leadership led to the restoration of our economy and the ultimate collapse of the Soviet Union. All of these things were deemed impossible and unrealistic, yet they were brought to fruition and America had risen to great new heights as a result. But how did President Reagan do it? How was he able to make America great again as he had sought?

One of the principles that defined President Reagan's character was his great sense of humility. He never assumed or accepted credit for the progress that was achieved during the 1980s; he accredited the American people as those who restored this country's greatness. He was absolutely correct! It is the people who hold this nation's fate, not the government. Our elected officials, however, are expected to serve us by setting the conditions for us to pursue our dreams and individual freedoms. They are expected also to remind us once in a while how special and unique we are as an exceptional society. President Reagan understood all of this very well, and all of his policies proved so. He knew that the cause for our suffering was at the fault of an overregulating, overspending, and overtaxing government. President Reagan was never ashamed to make it known, and he was surely not afraid to stick it into the face of the liberal Left. His primary goal was to remove government out of the way so the people could do what they have always done very best. He stood strongly for what he knew to be true and made it clear in every instance.

President Reagan never attempted to glorify the conventional professionalism or intellectualism for which most politicians do. He was not one of those who attempted time and again to fit in with everyone one. Instead he was a people person who understood the ordinary, everyday life of the common man. This is what makes President Reagan so exceptional in the eyes of many. He resonated with the American people so powerfully; he was surely one of us. He was not an advocate or supporter of the truly wealthy elite as the liberal Left and history books portray him to be. He believed that every person had the capability of achieving his or her dreams and control his or her own destiny. President Reagan not only loved America to the core, but proved it well through his policies and initiatives.

In the beginning I admired Ronald Reagan for his dynamic oratorical ability only. Through much studying and reading, I learned how and why President Reagan is indeed a hero; not just of America but the entire world. He was a phenomenal leader who restored the promise of this great nation when it seemed lost without a single trace. I will embrace and strive forever to carry on the vision he shared. I challenge everyone to not rely on textbooks or the media for learning who Ronald Reagan was, but investigate inside accounts such as his autobiography and a wonderful book entitled *Ronald Reagan: How an Ordinary Man Became an Extraordinary Leader.* He was not only a great president and leader, but the man who revived the spirit of America during one of her darkest hours.

Crisis in Leadership

You do not need me or the media to inform you constantly that our nation is in serious trouble. We are experiencing a very stagnant, unstable economy; the worst in many of our lifetimes. Millions of Americans remain without work, while millions more cannot afford a decent living. Children from all walks of life are being robbed of their future by a broken education system. The rising costs of healthcare continue to plague many Americans who are sick and in great need. Our nation's debt is the highest as it has ever been at seventeen trillion dollars; each one of our children in the future faces an average looming penalty of fifty thousand dollars and counting. Threats of radical Islamic terrorism and danger throughout the world continue to plague the lives of innocent individuals. We face a moral crisis that poses a solemn threat to our overall nation's stability. More important, our individual freedoms and God-given natural rights of Life, Liberty, and Pursuit of Happiness continue to be curtailed by an overreaching, intrusive government. Americans of every kind have lost the hope and confidence that the future can be one of greatness and opportunity. Some folks I am very close and dear at heart with have abandoned hope for recovery. People from all across the world continue to view us with cynicism and mockery.

Earlier on I asked a question: if America is the wonderful nation that many claim it to be in the midst of imperfection, then what is the problem? What is the reason for our sluggish economy, broken education system, ailing healthcare system, an astounding federal debt, and erosion of our constitutional liberties? Why has there been such a great loss of hope for what America can become? Before the answer is revealed, let us be reminded that none of this is our (the people's) fault. None of this is because we are living too well, spending too much, or because we have "too much" freedom. It is not because of gay people, immigrants, or those who are wealthy. The answer to the question at hand is very simple: an utter failure of leadership. One of the fundamental problems in the United States of America is a profound deficiency of leadership in Washington, D.C. The politicians in Washington are not worthy by any measure of being referred to as leaders.

They behave like leaders in no way, shape, or form. We hear so often of the importance of voting and making our voices heard on Election Day. While this is heavily important, I must point out that millions of individuals are discouraged from doing so even due to a politics that is severely broken. Americans continue to be discouraged and turned off by the lack of togetherness and bipartisanship among the people we have bestowed power.

Politicians in both parties have failed our great country and abandoned the vision that make us who we are as Americans. They continue to assume positions on issues that are poll-driven only, regardless of the enormity of the risks at stake. They have failed to make the difficult decisions that our future demands. The fact that which disturbs me the greatest is that they get to enjoy the privileges of a luxurious lifestyle and great wealth while millions of honest, hardworking American citizens are struggling deeply because of Washington's failed leadership. They enjoy the fancy homes and expensive vehicles while millions of Americans remain without work and progress. When a household has no stable structure, nothing will function in the manner in which it should. All of those within the household will be against one another, most likely. With no clear set of priorities, bills and expenses will go without payment, everyone will go out without food and water, and obligations will go unfulfilled. This may be able to sustain in the short-term, but the entire household will collapse as time progresses. The fall would not have been caused by external factors, but those from within. The very same situation is taking place in America today. It is a failure of our elected officials to act upon the significance of the issues at stake.

The politicians in Washington do not have to worry about paying the bills on time, purchasing enough food and water to last the entire month, and keeping up with the mortgage. They are not forced to stress over financing their children's college tuition, paying off personal debt, and securing loans from the bank. The people we elect into office do not feel the emotional suffering and discouragement as a result of economic shortcomings or the rising costs of gasoline. They do not understand the constant frustration and anger of individuals who cannot find work. The town of Washington, D.C. is out of touch with the American people and their struggles. No matter what may take place in the life of the honest, everyday American, the typical politician will stand safe and clear of crisis. They are far more concerned with poll percentages and odds for re-election instead of making the needed sacrifices to secure our future. The American people have the greatest discontentment and loss of faith in our government than at any other time in history. They are dissatisfied extremely and undeserving of the lack of leadership in Washington, and they have every right to be angry or upset.

I must reiterate the truth that the crises we face in this country are not at the fault of the American people by any measure. It is not because of too much technology or because some of us may be living too greatly. It is also important to dismiss the claim that the LGBT community or any other group of individuals stands at fault. Our crises exist due to a profound lack of vision and straightforwardness among those we have entrusted to represent us. The time has come for all of us to stand up and reverse this path we have traveled for far too long. We have answered the question that was at hand, which is a crisis in leadership in Washington, D.C. Now we must apply the long-term solutions to this problem.

What Makes a Leader

We discovered the reason we as Americans are experiencing great crisis, which is a lack of leadership from our elected officials. It is because they have profoundly forgotten =their purpose for power and have embarked upon a very dangerous course of partisanship and recklessness. At this point, we cannot refer to our elected officials as leaders, but instead politicians as we have concluded previously. The long-term interests and concerns of you and I have been abandoned. I feel with all of my heart we the American people can have far better if we are willing to reach deep into our hearts for the true qualities of a leader. We as Americans are obligated to know the principles of a true leader at heart. If we know how to define a leader, we can rid our government of all those who have taken America down the path she is on. Instead of relinquishing hope and confidence for the future, let us use this time as an opportunity to reclaim the leadership that will restore our nation's safeguards for the generations to come after.

All of us have our own convictions for what makes a dignified leader to the core. Although there is no right or wrong conviction, any one of them is better than those of what are in our nation's capital. For some time now, I have had the opportunity to serve many fellow young adults through leadership. I made it a duty to put the needs of everyone else before the needs of myself. It was a priority to treat others with the respect they deserved as human beings. I never once asked the question of what would I receive in return, but what would happen to everyone else if I did not fulfill my important obligations. The only time I would be satisfied is when the work of others was completed. At the end of the day, this was always the case. All of this, as well as wisdom from God, has taught me the true heart and character of a leader. I have faith that if these convictions are applied on Capitol Hill, we can finally lead our country on an upward path. There are five fundamental principles we must apply to leadership in America once more:

A) A personal, deep relationship with God.
B) Upholding the courage to pursue the difficult path which lies ahead.
C) Pursuing a vision that includes everyone as a whole.
D) Believing in people and their ability to overcome and prosper.
E) Seeking to bring both sides together in common purpose.

All that we are witnessing and have witnessed from our elected officials is clearly contrary to the principles listed above. The time is now for these principles of vision and leadership to be reapplied in Washington once more. Let us take this time to define each of these principles in great specific detail.

The beginning of true leadership begins with the vision and calling from God Himself. All of us are the children of God indeed; as His children, He should remain at the center of our lives so we do not lose His wisdom and spiritual hedge of protection. God intended for us to pursue wonderful, prosperous lives; but doing so begins with Him and nowhere else. God holds all of the knowledge that is bound to perfect lives and shape the world for the better. The only way to obtain this knowledge is through a relationship with Him. Leaders with a personal walk with God has the vision of greatness that God intends for us to live. He has the skills and tools for the fulfillment of His vision. A leader who has God at the center of His heart can be trusted to lead America in a very positive direction.

This is promoting religious affiliation or religion in general in no way, shape, or form. It also does not require a leader who would force any specific religion or religious principle on the American people, but someone with the personal character of God and His vision at heart. A fundamental part of God's character is putting the interests of others ahead of self and doing for others what is expected in return. The character of God also does not contain deceit and seeks to avoid major challenges through clarity. Many Godly ideals consist of character, integrity, humility, respect for others, and striving for peace. America requires someone who has lived and seen God's vision firsthand and is not ashamed to stand up for it. If a person loves and have faith in God truly, he or she is able to have faith in him- or herself and others. It is clear that the politicians in Washington are not Godly individuals; for they have deceived us by putting their own interests ahead of ours.

The second fundamental tenet of leadership is possessing the courage to pursue the difficult tasks which lie ahead. The problem in Washington is not defined by the lack of ability to do the people's work, but a failure of willingness in doing so. A person who has been called to serve others, whether in a major or minor aspect, must sit aside every short-term and personal interest. He or she have been assured the responsibility of fulfilling the people's work. Our government is obligated to do what the people cannot do themselves such as create the conditions for economic certainty, protect us from harm abroad, and manage infrastructure. Our elected officials are responsible for balancing the nation's budget and initiating policies that will strengthen our education system. Our children in future years will live in a world where they will be affected heavily by the decisions we make today. A leader with courage as well as integrity is not afraid to make tough, unpopular decisions when he may risk his opportunities for re-election. A true leader at heart will pursue politics not to advance his career but to better the lives of his fellow countrymen and -women.

Throughout many instances, leadership involves character assassination and personal ridicule. It involves countless hours of great discouragement and frustration. I have witnessed and endured much of this firsthand. I continued, however, to stand firmly for what I knew to be true and put people ahead of self. This is where the true test of leadership begins. Some individuals choose to surrender during their darkest hours; the majority of the politicians on Capitol Hill has done exactly that. Leaders understand the struggle is not personal; they understand that the task of representing the country demands thick skin and perseverance. No matter the scale of challenge the journey encounters, leaders do not compromise on the vision that must be pursued.

Some leaders are afraid to pursue the difficult road ahead, but fail to realize that many of the greatest individuals throughout history have done so regardless. Because they did, Americans for generations to come are better off. Due to their great courage and sacrifices through leadership, we are able to live better in contrast to previous generations in a very different world. President Reagan is the perfect example of a leader who did the people's work without excuse and stood strongly for what needed to be done in this country. It is time for our elected officials to rise above party and polls and politics and step up to the plate. A true, courageous leader will never fail to keep the best interests of people at heart no matter the circumstances.

The third critical tenet of leadership is pursuing a vision that includes everyone rather than one that recognizes some of the people as more or less important than others. This is one of the principles of leadership which always hits home for me. I demonstrate the most passion for this tenant for multiple reasons. First and foremost, each and every one of us is a child of God. We are all brothers and sisters of one another and have been given an equal share of beauty and uniqueness to share with the world. All of us are equal in the eyes of God and should, therefore, be so in the eyes of each other. A vision that includes all of the people is indifferent to race, color, gender, income level, sexual orientation, and religious affiliation.

Our destiny as an American people is shared; for we rise or fall as one and one only. Any person in America who would regard someone differently due to the color of his or her skin or how much he or she makes per year or who he or she chooses to love is not worthy of and does not belong in a position of power. A leader at heart does not show special treatment in an effort to pick up votes to win an election; neither will he or she attempt to divide individuals into members of hyphenated groups or classes. Pursuing a vision of such is anathema to everything we believe in and stand for here in America.

Our nation has been divided into many aspects; rich and poor, gay and straight, men and women, black and white, conservative and liberal, and pro-life and pro-choice. A true American leader does not feed into this tendency to differentiate the American people. Leaders acknowledge the greatness in everyone and builds upon it. They initiate policies that ensures opportunity for all Americans to succeed; they seek to establish equal treatment for everyone in the eyes of the law. In addition to a failure of leadership in Washington, D.C., one of the reasons our country is on a stagnant path is our tendency to create differences in one another and attack each other because we disagree with them.

Leaders will not pursue initiatives such as affirmative action or policies that discriminate against the LGBT community or economic policies that penalize and discourage individuals and families earning a certain income each year. Leaders will never abandon any person or persons and leave them behind. They will seek the betterment of each and every single American by working towards a future where all are regarded with the respect and dignity they deserve as human beings. I refuse to settle for elected officials who choose to regard some Americans in a positive or negative light due to what they look like or the amount of money they earn or who they choose to share eternity with; America requires leaders who sees all of the people of this great nation as individuals as well as the equal children of God.

The fourth important tenet of leadership is believing in people and their ability to achieve the American Dream. A leader who believes in people puts forth initiatives that empowers individuals to be strong as well as responsible and self-sufficient; he or she will not pursue policies that discourages drive and confidence and encourages dependency and entitlement. Leaders will seek to initiate policies that ensure the equality of opportunity to succeed versus the effort to compel an equality of outcomes. They will preserve the freedom for each and every American to lead his or her life the way he or she feels is best. Leaders will not seek to advance the welfare state or coerce the hands of government in our lives in a way that was unintended. They will heed the words of Lincoln when he proclaimed that men cannot be helped permanently when things are done for them that could and should done by them. True, honest leaders with integrity understand that people are better off in the long-term when they are filled with purpose and the drive to achieve their dreams. They will establish policies that make it simpler for the free market and private enterprise to thrive by rewarding determination and risk-taking. Leaders will not discourage free enterprise by raising tax rates and increasing government regulations and restrictions. They will work to empower young people to achieve their potential and be productive men and women of society.

Leadership is not looking someone in the eye asking for trust, but by encouraging him or her to trust in the power within him or her bestowed by God. The politicians in Washington, liberals primarily, have been attempting to make more and more individuals subservient to government through either victimization or servitude. Leaders will never exploit an individual's frustration and anger; they stand by people and lead them in achieving their dreams and heart-set desires.

The fifth and final tenet of leadership is bringing both sides together with a common goal. All Americans would agree that the major problem on Capitol Hill is the profound inability of elected officials to unite in solving the major challenges we face. Never before in our history has this taken place in the magnitude in which it has since President Obama assumed the Oval Office. Both parties are guilty of failing to do what needs to be done to heal our nation. The politicians in Washington persist with the constant back-and-forth bickering and refusal to compromise on minor proposals instead of sitting personal gain aside and doing what is best for America. A leader to the core at heart is able to stand passionately for what he or she knows to be true yet rise to a higher occasion when time demands it. He or she will not mistake party line or political label for excuses to not reach out to the other side. A leader cares more for the better of his country than loyalty to his party; he knows how to bridge divides and establish togetherness. All things we do in our lives demand compromise at times; our friendships, partnerships, relationships, etc. A leader is never afraid to stand up to his or her own base or party when time demands it; he sees disagreement as an opportunity to advance ideas and proposals to lead our nation forward.

America is not only in crisis; she is experiencing a period of great change. I will explore this change in greater detail throughout future chapters. I can say now, however, that the change we are witnessing demands more seriousness than ever from our elected officials. It will demand courage to abandon the child play, come together, and offer a bold agenda to solve the challenges of our time.

The Difficult Journey Ahead

The challenges we face as an American people are as critical and serious as they have ever been. Americans are suffering from the loss of work, failing schools, lack of healthcare, a rising federal debt, etc. Our world has become as dangerous as it had been during the Cold War. Our society is experiencing a moral crisis and breakdown of the family. America is suffering from gun violence like never before. Our constitutional freedoms and God-given rights of Life, Liberty, and the Pursuit of Happiness continue to be threatened by the overreach of big government.

Today's generation has been called upon to make a fundamental choice for our nation's future: a fundamental choice between weakness and strength; division and togetherness; bewilderment and discernment; and pessimism and hope. We are a strong and generous people; we are the envy of the world; and we consist of the most exceptional society ever known to the face of mankind. The United States has overcome every crisis there is from economic collapse to racial discrimination to the terrible scourge of communism. We have long risen to the demands of destiny and shaped it like no other, but there lies great work before us. I have faith that we the American people will not only restore leadership, but stand firm and walk tall and never relent in choosing the right path for America.

"You cannot escape the responsibility of tomorrow by evading it today."

~President Abraham Lincoln

Chapter 4

A Nation that Prospers

I will never forget the days as a child growing up on the north side of Chicago. Our family was poor; living paycheck to paycheck. There would be little or no food in our home on most days. It was not very often when I was able to receive video games or toys. Like so many families all across America, we were forced to wait until Christmas time or tax return season to afford certain luxuries and many of the things we desired. This was difficult for me to accept and understand as a small child growing up. My mom forever did her very best to instill in me the importance in getting an education and reaching for the greater things in life. I was reminded of this every time I passed up a fancy home or an expensive-looking vehicle on the street. As I became much older, I realized that the world is such a vast place with limitless opportunities. It is a place where I learned I can fulfill every dream in my heart. Instead of envying others for having more than myself, I began to set major goals for the future.

The only reason certain individuals can afford fancy real estate, expensive vehicles, and lavish clothing is that they did what was needed to be done to have the desires of their hearts. They did not rely on handouts from government; they were not victims of circumstances and did not allow the obstacles before them to get the best of them. I realized the exact same can happen in my life if I apply every effort to achieve the American Dream. I thought about my wife and children in the future and vowed to give them a far greater life than the one I lived as a child. One of the most valuable lessons I learned as a teenager was that strong values and faith in God and self will carry an individual as far as he or she could ever imagine. My dreams, hopes, and goals for a prosperous life are possible because I have a God who loves us all very much and I live in a nation where anything is possible.

An American Dream for Everyone

For the past two centuries, millions of people from all over the world have come here to America with hopes of leading a greater life. They desired to extend a legacy of prosperity and greatness to their children and so on. Many of these individuals emigrated from countries throughout Central America and Europe and Asia where it is nearly impossible to fulfill dreams and hopes. Government tells people how much money they will earn, the amount of property they can own, and how to conduct their personal lives. It owns practically all of the means of production and assumes the majority of private capital. If someone is not in association with a certain family or was not born into wealth or promise, there are no possible methods of breaking the cycle of poverty because the opportunity to rise higher does not exist. Citizens in these countries do not have the freedom to set the course for their lives because government believes they are not capable and smart enough to do so. This has left many without food, homes, water, and, most of all, hope. Many of us here in America could never imagine how to endure such conditions.

A great number of people in these societies come here to the United States to escape this kind of tyranny and despair where it is nearly impossible to live their dreams and lead a better life. They could have never chosen such a better place to escape than right here in the land of opportunity. The reality here in America is far unique; someone who is struggling through the absolute worst of circumstances and has nothing more except for the clothes on his or her back can have far greater and beyond. A small business struggling to obtain capital and vital resources can rise to Fortune 500 and be traded publicly on Wall-Street. A young person who comes from the poorest of families can live up to the highest expectations and ideals and offer more to his or her children in the future.

It is the dream of every American to have great luxury and limitless wealth. There is absolutely no shame or harm for an individual to feel such a way; this is one of the underlying principles that makes America exceptional and great. When an entrepreneur creates and expands a business, employment is expanded for those looking for work and opportunity is extended to climb the ladder of successful achievement. Every employee has the opportunity to become employer through self-determination and hard work. When an individual achieves success, it spreads to others. This is what hails free enterprise as the single most powerful engine of opportunity and prosperity in the world. It has been always and will be forever. The possession of great wealth should not be frowned upon in America. It should be admired and encouraging rather, so as long as it is achieved through honesty and humility. This is the reason millions of individuals from all across the world come here to our blessed, wonderful land.

Every person can succeed in America through self-assurance and striving to overcome any and all obstacles. The notion that skin color and background are permanent barriers is deliberately misleading. If some were to observe, they would realize there are Americans of every kind who have broken the shackles of poverty and despair and rose to heights unforeseen. The American Dream has never been based upon color or circumstance, but character; not race, but responsibility; not envy of wealth, but equality of opportunity for every single American. There should consist of no classes or groups of individuals in this great country. There should be no "99 percent" or "1 percent", but total recognition of 100 percent of the American people. Instead of dividing us from another in terms of how we look and how much we make each year, there should be each and every American with a dream to have more and the drive and opportunity to achieve it. There should be no American considered more or less important than any other on the basis of income, skin color, gender, etc.

There are two kinds of people in America who will struggle; there are those Americans who will struggle from circumstances beyond their control such as a declining economy, a broken healthcare system, a failing education system, and a stagnant housing market as well as the overreach of intrusive government, and there are those Americans who will struggle by their own means. Those who will struggle by their own means do so because of certain decisions they have made in the past and/or are making in the present. Many of these individuals blame others for their situations and choose to believe they are entitled to the American Dream with no hard work and determination; therefore, they cannot be served with long-term assistance until they change their attitude and methods of decision-making. They do not have the right to live off of those who have fulfilled or are fulfilling their God-given desires. The millions of Americans who are just making ends meet or out of work due to an ailing economy deserve a greater shot at the American Dream. All of the children attending failing schools deserve a far better opportunity at a decent education. The businesses that are struggling to obtain capital can achieve greater success without the many arbitrary regulations and rules and high taxation.

I believe with all of my heart we can expand opportunity to every American who is struggling from this ailing economy as well as circumstances beyond his or her own control. I believe we can create a new and lasting foundation for an economy that rewards success and hard work instead of punishing it. We can re-connect all of those who have abandoned their American Dream with the hope to achieve it fully.

Across-the-Board Tax Relief

There is a great debate in America concerning who deserves lower tax rates and how our tax code should be reformed. All of us know the Left's position on taxes in this country; time and time again they have advocated more and more taxes on those who have accumulated great wealth. Liberals believe it will do well in the long-term to the individuals who have yet to achieve their American Dream to punish those who have. We have seen throughout history that this has not only failed to do so, but it discourages business growth and investment here in America. Despite what the Democratic leadership and liberal media have proclaimed, why do you think so many goods and services are now being manufactured on the opposite of the world? The top tax rate in our country during the 1930s was over sixty percent. Many of the rising Hollywood actors at this time began to go overseas to progress their careers.

The tax rate on high-income earners would remain about the same until the days of President Reagan. The rate was reduced to twenty-eight percent, while many Americans in lower tax brackets were exempt from paying federal income taxes entirely. Our economy skyrocketed from the deepest crisis since the Great Depression to the strongest in the world. America saw the rise of science and high technology as well as the creation of nineteen million new jobs. President Reagan proved we are all Americans with the dream to pursue greatness and made it clear that anyone of us can live our dreams. He knew that pitting the American people against one another would not solve the problem but worsen it. President Reagan knew also that punishing success and wealth stands against every principle upon which America was established.

The Left's philosophy of punishing success and re-distributing wealth does not live up to history and has failed to create opportunity. It does not only hurt those who are rich, but all of those Americans who are trying simply to earn a living. When businesses have to pay more in taxes, the prices of goods and services rise while the wages of hardworking men and women plummet. Higher taxes also take away money that businesses could invest to create more jobs. This is unmitigated common sense. So what is the best, most efficient way to reform our federal income tax code? How do we rid the tax code of all loopholes and special giveaways? What must be done to allow every hardworking American to keep more of their money? We must realize, first and foremost, it is not necessary to increase tax rates on some in order to provide relief for others. All of us believe in the American Dream, work very hard to achieve it, and have families. Every American who earns a source of income deserves to keep most of it.

The very first approach to simplifying America's tax system must consist of the removal of all personal exemptions and deductions. Secondly we must scrap the current progressive tax code and replace it with a simple, proportional across-the-board flat-tax. Finally, we must reduce the overall rate in taxes paid by every American to 10 percent. Once we simplify the individual income tax code, there will be the need for tax credits and special rewards no longer. No American would be penalized for making over a certain amount of money or be allowed to abuse the tax code by not paying his or her fair share. If someone makes $25,000, he or she would pay $2,500 in taxes; if an individual makes $100,000, he or she would pay $10,000; if he or she earns $250,000, he or she would pay $25,000 in federal income taxes. We must reduce the corporate tax rate from 35 percent to 20 percent so America can compete better globally. There should be an elimination of taxes on capital gains so businesses can expand and spread opportunity right here in the United States. Furthermore, there must be bipartisanship in Congress in deciding on a final package based on these principles. We must focus on a goal of more taxpayers rather more taxes.

The very last thing we as Americans should do is settle for the broken, failed tax code we have today. It is counterproductive economically and continues to rob millions of individuals and families of their hard-earned money. The Left realizes this completely, but chooses to not change course. Liberals on Capitol Hill believe government knows better how to manage the people's money than the people themselves; they would rather see more Americans give up their money rather than keep it to support their families, enjoy their accomplishments, and build their communities. This is not the American Dream as you or I know it.

What the Left fails to realize is that the current progressive system allows some with higher incomes to pursue fraud and abuse by refusing to pay a fair share. It also encourages them to invest their money overseas to avoid paying higher rates, which only counters economic growth here in this country. If America is to prosper at full throttle, we must have a tax code where every American is treated justly and rewarded for their hard work and sacrifice. In the wealthiest nation on Earth where dreams are valued and opportunity is vibrant, it should not be made impossible for individuals to live up to their highest expectations and prosper to the fullest.

Restructuring America's Education System

The greatest long-term challenge America faces is our broken education system. This issue will forever hit home with me. All of us know very well that a great education opens many doors of opportunities for which are nearly impossible without the completion of school. The higher level of education an individual has, the more successful he or she is likely to become. Education provides more than just certification to perform certain jobs; it nurtures the intellectual ability to transform lives for the better and perfect the world we live in. It would be a moral injustice to rob our children of the greatest opportunity to do so. A great education leads the effort in fulfilling the American Dream. Many of the distinguished men and women who have come before us completed both high-school and college and gave their all to extend this legacy to us.

The issue of education is a very key factor in the eradication of poverty as well as in solidifying our long-term economic strength. We cannot expect to remain the center of the world's prosperity if we do not reform our education system. It is not rocket science to figure out the system is in great crisis. I have witnessed it first hand with great frustration and anger. I had the opportunity to speak at a number of schools and sought the opinions of many teachers and faculty members as well as students. I was appalled to the core by so many of the regulations and restrictions for which exist. Most of them are over-burdensome yet senseless and unnecessary. They discourage many well-intended, hardworking teachers and students from giving their absolute best. While many of the rules consist of a combination of federal, state, and local laws, most of them stem from the federal government to the states and carried out by local school boards. All of us are very aware of the long-term negative effects that are caused by the act of overregulating, which include many long hours of extra unnecessary work and the demoralizing of hardworking, dedicated men and women, as well as the failure of services in being fulfilled.

I began to witness the crisis in education first hand as a student in high-school and as a speaker. I was very close with my content mastery instructor. I will never forget the many days when he was forced to complete paperwork instead of assisting his students as he preferred. He claimed No Child Left Behind as the reason he attended to so much paperwork. The situation became no better under Race to the Top, and it becomes very much worse in Louisiana with its broken education system. In Louisiana, teachers are obligated to divide their students into groups and insist they "teach themselves". Teachers are instructed on how to teach their students rather than use the methods they know well already. This is the very reason they attended college for four or more years. No person seeks four years of training and certification for a task just to be told how to perform it afterwards. Students are affected negatively as well; they are unable to receive the proper education required if their teachers cannot assist them as needed.

An additional issue for which requires attention is the discipline system. If a student misbehaves during class, the teacher is not allowed to send him or her out of the classroom. As the teacher spends half of class time attending to the misbehavior of a particular student, the others are being neglected from much-needed information they should be learning. Furthermore, this sends a message to the misbehaving student that there are no consequences for his or her actions. Once again, these are some of the restrictions imposed by the federal government, enforced by the states, and carried out by local school boards.

While I am not fully certain of the effects of America's education crisis elsewhere, I am frustrated and disappointed beyond a doubt of the aftermath in the parish I live in central Louisiana. So many talented and wonderful teachers have either retired or transferred to other parishes, test scores and overall student performance have declined, and general discipline is beyond horrific. One of my closest friends, who I consider a brother-in-Christ, was fired in 2011 because of the way he carried out his lesson plans. An additional friend, who is a teacher at the school from which I had graduated, informed me that many remaining teachers have become so stressed they had begun consuming anti-depressant medications. I learned also that the school lunches are not very good, and parents are not allowed to send their children to school with their own lunches. For the past three years, less than twenty-five percent of students in the parish I live succeeded in passing the state assessment test. More than half of all classrooms are filled with substitute teachers who know very little about the subjects they are assigned, teaching in general, and helping students prepare for the future.

Millions of students in cities and towns all across America are forced to attend failing schools where they are being robbed of their shot at the American Dream. I continue to pray each and every night for not only these children but mine and others in the years to come. I pray not in anger and frustration but confidence and faith. Our children requires more than just prayers and hope, however. They deserve progress; they deserve schools where they are able to learn and achieve the best possible education. It must be the fundamental priority of us all to help every child fulfill his or her God-given potential. Every child deserves an education system that puts them and their needs before all else. The current system is broken; it is failing our teachers, students, and communities.

America during one point in history ranked first in the number of college graduates, reading and math scores, and science and high-technology. Government spent nearly seven-hundred billion dollars on education within 2009-10, yet the system fails to improve. We cannot afford to continue adapting the same failed ideas over and over again, thinking the system will improve. The clock will tick eventually if we do not begin to change course today. The fundamental cause of America's education crisis is the overreach of government through national standards and arbitrary regulations. An additional factor is the failure to emphasize the importance of technology and science. There are four specific goals we must strive to meet in the effort to set America's education system on a higher path:

A) Return education to the authority of the states, local school boards, and parents.
B) Abolish all forms of standardized testing and ACT
C) Initiate voucher system for charter and parochial schools.
D) Encourage and empower relationships between teachers, students, and parents.

The problem with Washington is it believes greater power and more control are the solutions to our nation's challenges. The flip side to government funding is the attachment of strings. When a school receives federal funding, it must comply with specific rules and standards; if the school fails to comply, it loses its funding. The problem in America's education system is not money, but a lack of policies that reflect competence and common sense. I understand the motivation beneath the position for national standards; however, it is not in our best interests long-term to impose the same standards for every school across the country. Each community in America stands differently from others; therefore, various communities require specific means for which certain goals are obtained. The same principle applies someone who is sick, which some patients require different medications than others. The priority of education must be returned to the hands of states and local communities, with the exception for financial student aid for college.

People in their own states and communities know better better how to run and manage their schools and educate their children, unlike government bureaucrats thousands of miles away who know nothing about children and education. Teachers know very well how the classroom should be ran and should be in control of running it. When a student misbehaves and causes disruption, he or she must be dealt with the proper consequences. Parents must have the choice of sending their children to school with lunches of their own, and the new national standards for school lunches should be eliminated. There is no single bureaucrat in this country who knows better than parents and teachers how to educate and prepare our children for the future.

We must seek also to abolish all forms of standardized testing as well as the ACT. This principle continues to resonate with me as it has since high-school. I have always felt very strongly that state-sponsored standardized testing is rather a diversion than an asset for training students to succeed. Much of the material on standardized tests are not covered in the classroom, yet passage or failure depends on our knowledge of the material. From personal experience, I have never felt smarter or better about my future after completing a state-sponsored test. In fact I never performed too well on them as hard as I attempted. I performed well enough on the ACT to qualify for a college scholarship, which amounted to very little. I ran out of time before I was able to complete the test in full. I was disappointed that I did not earn a score high to enter into the university I desired. My grade point average upon graduation, however, was a 3.8. I never ceased to excel and learn as much as I possibly could during class time. I realized I could not hold my position on my own experience alone. As time went on, I received the perspectives of other students as well as teachers. I became astonished somewhat in learning the burden was just as great on teachers, principals, and school board officials as it was on students.

Throughout my time in school, I learned how significant teacher-student/parent relationships can be. I learned also that a student's education is best served by what he or she received in the classroom. There must be very strong emphasis on reaching into the heart of each and every student. We need to begin the process of helping every child develop his or her God-given potential. Teachers must reach out to both the student and parent to determine the student's strengths and possible methods to overcome his or her weaknesses. Parents must know how their children are performing in the classroom. Teachers and parents must hold each other accountable; if one alone does not fulfill the much needed obligations, the student will suffer.

Instead of wasting time and resources and spending billions of dollars each year on standardized testing, let us begin to invest in programs at the state and local level that specializes in specific career fields to assist students in developing and applying their potential. It is not in the best interests of students for us to wait until they reach college to invest in their talents and goals. The student should be exposed to training and career assessments all throughout high-school and ready to excel to college afterwards. The passage of career assessments and training, controlled and ran locally, should serve as the replacement for the ACT and SAT. By a student's junior year in high-school, he or she should have a very general idea of his or her career choice for later on.. A student's acceptance into college should be based partly on what he or she has learned in the classroom as well as pre-readiness for his or her career; it should not be based on a test with material irrelevant to his or her future that has not been taught. Not only will taxpayer dollars be saved and used for greater efficient initiatives, our children will be served well in their endeavor to fulfill their American Dream.

As we build to improve America's education system, we must give parents the choice to send their children to better schools where they will have greater opportunities to succeed. It will take more than a good night's sleep to overcome the crisis in our public school system here in America. Progress will not be short nor simple; the task will be long and difficult. There will be major setbacks and obstacles that will lead to discouragement and great disappointment. Our children in failing schools should not be asked to settle and/or wait for the system to be fixed. Every low-income family should be afforded a one-time voucher to send their children to a charter or parochial school of their choosing. The voucher program should be initiated at the state level to increase flexibility and save money at the federal level.

It strikes me a great deal how many on the Left would force America's children to settle for the failed system we have currently, yet fail to reverse the course of direction. In my current hometown in central Louisiana, the school board continues to push back against vouchers in order to maintain funding for the failing public schools. Sometimes I wonder when they will realize that failure will not be overcame by pouring more and more money into a failed system. The problem is caused not by a lack of money, as stated earlier on, but incompetency and over-burdensome red-tape imposed by the federal government.

There is far too much at stake for us to choose money and the failed status quo over our children's future. Every family living at or below the poverty line should be given a voucher of at least a thousand dollars or more to go out and choose a charter or parochial school they feel will offer their children an honest and decent shot at pursuing their God-given potential. The voucher is critically important because most of the children in failing public schools consist of families living in poverty. The expectations for these children to break the cycle of poverty are too great, and their families deserve the chance to do so. Our children deserve support as they seek to build a better life for themselves and their children in future years. If we intend to spread opportunity and strengthen the American Dream for generations to come, we must apply these principles to America's education system so our children can have a shot to prosper to the fullest extent.

Return to Fiscal Stability in America

In his farewell address to the nation on September 17, 1796, President George Washington spoke these words:
"As a very important source of strength and security, cherish public credit. One method of preserving it is, to use it as sparingly as possible; avoiding occasions of expense by cultivating peace, but remembering also that timely disbursements to prepare for danger frequently prevent much greater disbursements to repel it; avoiding likewise the accumulation of debt, not only by shunning occasions of expense, but by vigorous exertions in time of peace to discharge the debts, which unavoidable wars may have occasioned, not ungenerously throwing upon posterity the burthen, which we ourselves ought to bear."

The national debt in the United States as of the year 1796 was 83,762,172 dollars and 7 cents. It would remain consistent on average over the next half of century. As the second half of the Nineteenth Century approached, our debt as a nation began to skyrocket. Fast-forwarding to the first year of the Millennium, America was enjoying a record budget surplus of 236.2 billion dollars. We were on the path to pay off our nation's debt in full, as well as ensuring the solvency of Social Security and Medicare. This was a time of high economic certainty in our country; expanded from the expansion which took place during the 1980s. There was a sense of great confidence and optimism for the future. Over the past decade and a half, this wonderful period has declined as the result of a financial collapse, international turmoil, declining incomes, and, most of all, a rising national debt. Our debt rises little by little each and every second that proceeds. America's debt, as of this moment, is estimated to be 17,596,911,200,000 dollars. How long do you feel it would take to walk along over seventeen trillion bodies on an open field? What would spark inside of your mind about the reality of such a large number?

The worst act we could make as Americans is to underestimate the size and scope of our nation's debt as well as the significance behind it. Our entire future stands at enormous risk on this single issue alone. Each and every person in this country owes an estimated count of 55,200 dollars to the federal government, while every taxpayer owes an estimated amount of 151,000 dollars. It is abundantly clear that America is in the midst of the worst fiscal crisis in our history. The crisis will only worsen for our children and grandchildren in many years to come. The Congressional Budget Office has projected the debt to exceed our nation's entire output by the year 2039. This means we will owe more money than we are producing in the overall economy, which poses a very dangerous risk to America's future. There are millions of Americans who continue to wonder if our debt can or will be repaid. The American people have enough trouble seeking to repay their own debt individually; the last thing they deserve is a double burden.

Our nation is suffering from a serious case of out-of-control spending in Washington. Before we can pursue the path to fiscal responsibility in America and extend our children a future of security and certainty, we must know what led us to the current situation from the beginning. There is a great debate taking place in Washington of whether or not we are suffering from a revenue problem or spending problem. No matter which you may believe to be true, both Republicans and Democrats are to blame for our current crisis. Both parties have raised the debt ceiling on countless occasions, expanded the power of government, and continue to spend trillions of dollars we do not have on programs proven again and again to be counterproductive. I cannot reiterate enough the very dangerous course path our government has led us to. Millions of seniors face the risk of losing their social security and Medicare, our veterans stand the chance of losing their benefits, and millions of Americans across-the-board face the risk of mass increases in tax rates. Government continues to spend hundreds of billions of dollars on growing the welfare state; it continues to borrow trillions of dollars from countries such as China and India to build other nations instead of our own.

For far too long now, the federal government has assumed responsibilities it was never intended by our Founding Fathers to assume. It has taken on education, urban development, environmental protection, etc. All of these are issues that affect people on an individual and personal level. The same rules and standards may not apply for every single individual or area. This is one of the very reasons states, cities, and local communities were intended to handle such issues. State and local leaders know the area better and the people in the area. The reality of one place may be completely different from that of another place. If states, cities, and local communities take most of the responsibility for these initiatives, the costs would be far less expensive. The outcome would result in greater long-term efficiency and success.

We have seen the failed results again and again of the many attempts made by the federal government to grow beyond its constitutional boundaries. Our government was created to perform duties authorized by the Constitution only. All of those duties can be summed up in three specific tasks, as I listen in the recent chapter; create the framework for economic successful achievement, protect the nation from harm abroad, and promote the equal treatment of all individuals regardless of who they are. These are three things we as Americans cannot do ourselves; the federal government plays the fundamental role in all three.

If we seek to eliminate wasteful spending and reduce our nation's debt truly, government must prioritize. It must be reminded of its constitutional purposes intended from the beginning. There are some things it does, however, that are greatly beneficial such as student financial aid for college, Headstart, Medicare, Social Security, and the Children's National Health Insurance. These programs must remain indeed. In the effort to reduce waste and fraud, government must use a scalpel to eliminate what does not work. After identifying what is important but ran poorly, leaders must determine the most smooth and efficient manner to transfer power and authority to state and local governments.

There must be limits and restrictions in place to receive welfare and unemployment benefits, such as drug tests and deadlines for employment. Because this program is paid for by honest, hardworking taxpayers, there must be integrity and competency in the system. Congress must pass and states must amend a balanced-budget amendment to the Constitution to ensure that government live within its means. Congress must pass a line-item veto for the President to stamp out waste and overspending without vetoing an entire bill that may contain valuable and positive appropriations. Congress must adopt Pay-As-You-Go once more to ensure that initiatives are paid for and not kicked down the road to future generations. There must be a special task force appointed by the President, consisting of both Democrats and Republicans, to identify specific long-term mechanisms to reduce our nation's overall debt.

This is a very delicate situation; the slightest mistake or miscalculation could induce major repercussions. Our children's future stands at major risk, as well as our nation's long-term stability. If America takes the bold, swift actions that are required, I feel with all of my heart that our debt crisis can be overcame and we can balance the budget and produce record surpluses for years to come.

Securing America's Future

All of us in this country wish nothing but the best for ourselves and our children. We hope for them a future where all of their dreams and heart-set desires can be achieved through hard work and self-determination. If we are to ask ourselves: what must each of us do to help our children become all they can be? What must be done for the American Dream to be uplifted for everyone and secured for all of those to come after? The United States has more wealth and freedom than any nation on Earth. We are the single most prosperous society in the world in spite of economic uncertainties.

Have we ever really taken the time to discover the igniting force beneath our prosperity and power? It is that good old American spirit. The American spirit is what makes us who we are. It inspires each of us to reach for the stars in the face of horrific possibilities. It empowers us to overcome our struggles and every challenge that gets in our way. The good old American spirit reminds us that we are all in this together regardless of color, background, gender, and income level. It encourages us to fight so that all of our wonderful children can inherit a future where they can stand strong, walk tall with their heads set forward, and strive for a better tomorrow.

"Our deep spiritual confidence that this nation will survive the perils of today – which may well be with us for decades to come – compels us to invest in our nation's future, to consider and meet our obligations to our children and the numberless generations that will follow."

~President John F. Kennedy

Chapter 5

A World at Peace

I will never forget the early morning of September 11, 2001 when one of our most beloved cities was under attack. It was the first time in nearly sixty years that American soil would face an attack by a foreign entity. I was six years old only on the day of the attacks on 9/11. There was no way possible for me of understanding the significance beneath the event. All I knew was two airplanes crashed into the World Trade Towers in New York City. I awoke to the sight of two burning buildings on the television screen, knowing not of the reason. I was aware of the attack on the Pentagon also.

At the time, I did not know whether or not if the plane crashes were accidental or deliberate. Eventually, on this day, the truth of a terrorist plot would be confirmed. It took some years for me to begin to learn of and understand the reality of what had taken place on 9/11. As my world view began to mold, the significance and reasoning behind the events on September 11, 2001 became abundantly clear. I realized, furthermore, our protection and security here at home is the most important aspect of our nation's strength and stability. It is either willful ignorance or a pure lack of understanding if one would believe we should cower away from our responsibilities to our national defense in the pursuit of maintaining America's safety and security. It is also a dangerous thing if we support the belief that America should not maintain a dynamic role in spreading democracy and peace throughout the world.

The Ash Heap of History

America will carry forever the horrors of the Cold War Era. It will be remembered always as the most defining challenge of America's strength and resolve. The slightest misuse of military action or diplomacy could have resulted in major catastrophe, which would have resulted in the loss of millions of lives. The Soviet Union was a very dangerous force of evil during the mid-Twentieth Century. It was growing at a rapid paste in pursuit of global domination. It seemed to have surpassed the United States with greater nuclear capability by 1960. I have heard many stories of the times when children in school were taught to slouch behind their desks in case of a nuclear bomb threat. Millions of Americans lived each day in fear; for the threat of nuclear catastrophe was possible at any given time. Communist totalitarianism served as the greatest threat to every aspect of mankind on Earth. It saw the deaths of millions who showed resistance. Under communism, government controlled where a person worked, how long someone worked, the amount of one's income, and where he or she lived. All businesses, property, and means of production were operated and controlled by the state.

This Marxist-socialist philosophy was anathema to the principles and ideals we have stood for in America strongly for nearly two-hundred, forty years. It has left many behind in poverty and despair, with no hope for a greater tomorrow. There is no way we as Americans could ever imagine what it was like to live in the Soviet Union during the Cold War Era. However, there was the possibility for America and many more nations to become the same if we did not rise to the challenge and take the Soviet Union head on.

We did that exactly under the leadership of President Reagan. President Reagan succeeded in eight years what seven leaders before him had failed to do in thirty five, which was bring the Soviet Union to its knees and communist totalitarianism to its ultimate demise. Leftist intellectuals and the mainstream media reported time and time again that America's best days were behind her and the Soviet Union would become the world's dominant force of leadership.

The Left told us again and again how dangerous it would be for America to stand toe-to-toe with the Soviet Union. Those on the Left claimed to be advocates for peace, but saw weakness and appeasement as the means to achieve it. It is just as saying I deserve respect from everyone else but feel as if I am not obligated to return the favor. No matter the cost, President Reagan did not compromise on principle by relenting from the challenges beforehand. He knew America possessed every bit of strength that was required to overcome the might of the Soviet Union and the grave threat of communist totalitarianism.

So how was President Reagan able to win the Cold War for America in the 1980s? What strategy did he use to bring the Soviet empire to its knees? It is extremely complex to understand how this was possible. Millions of both American and Soviet lives were at stake during the time before the Cold War was brought to a close. As many can recall, America and the Soviet Union were engaged in a major arms race for the world's nuclear arsenal. There were countless calls from the Left to end America's build-up of arms, as well as a proposal from General Secretary Gorbachev. Mr. Gorbachev promised to end the Soviet's build-up if America did so first. This was seen by the Left as a possible end to the Cold War and the beginning of peace once and for all; however, it would have stood as an act of appeasement on the part of America. There was no promise the Soviets would reduce their nuclear build-up if we did so first. For all we knew, it could have been a deliberate set up on the part of the Soviets in order to lead the build-up.

President Reagan vowed to resume the arms race with the Soviet Union. In addition to avoiding appeasement and weakness, he continued the build-up of nuclear weapons here at home for a very critical purpose. The Soviet Union was experiencing a period of economic decline. This was a classic example of socialist economic failure. Nations throughout history have always sought to strengthen their military might in times of economic vulnerability. Because the economy is weak and cannot serve as the fundamental source of national strength, nations bestow greater emphasis on their national defense in hope of remaining stable. President Reagan recognized this as a great opportunity to destroy the Soviets' overall strength. The longer the nuclear arms race sustained, the more capital the Soviets would invest in military power. The more money the Soviets invested in the arms race, the weaker the Soviet economy became.

President Reagan knew this extremely well and did not hesitate to capitalize on such a grand opportunity. Because he believed in America and stood face-to-face to the Soviet empire, the wrath of communist totalitarianism was met with defeat and the threat of nuclear catastrophe was finally over. America also helped release countries such as Grenada and many more from Soviet totalitarian control and returned them to democracy. The world entered a new era of peace and stability where the evil of communism conquered no more.

America's Role: Leader of the World

For nearly a century, the United States has stood very strongly as the greatest force of freedom and hope for all of the world. While great chaos and evil remains throughout the world today, many regions throughout the globe are far better off due to America's leadership. Nations such as Grenada, Costa Rica, Ukraine, and many others have witnessed the flames of democracy and liberty. The sacred state of Israel, our closest and greatest ally, remains secure and safe because of the United States. It was our leadership that defeated the regime of Nazi Germany and fascism throughout Europe. And, of course, America, through the courageous leadership of President Reagan, defeated the Soviet totalitarian regime.

We saw the results in the early 1900s when America pursued an isolationist path after World War I. If we would have maintained our leadership, Hitler's regime would have never become as strong as it did in Germany. The Holocaust would have never taken place, and millions of lives could have been spared. There was a great debate over the legacy of the war in Vietnam. Many people believed America's involvement in the war was a complete and utter failure. It became clear that our intentions to contain communism in North Vietnam and establish a free and democratic South Vietnamese state became curtailed. This was a result partly of the French surrender and withdrawal from the war. Our fundamental objective in Vietnam was to help bring about freedom and liberty to those inflicted by the spread of communism.

America's role has always been to help make the world more secure and peaceful and free; this was the case exactly in Vietnam. Our troops did not deserve the ridicule and persecution they received upon returning home. While our goal in Vietnam was not achieved, we must acknowledge the seriousness in defeating the Domino Effect. This was one failed battle in overcoming the communist regime; our men and women deserve great praise and appreciation for sacrificing their lives in the name of freedom.

We must never mistake America's role in the world as policing every wrong that takes place. America should refrain from simple conflicts between nations that do not pose a threat to us or countless lives. However, we must take a stand in certain instances where millions of lives stand in harm's way. This was the justification behind America's killing of Muammar Gaddafi, Hosni Mubarak, and, most importantly, Osama bin Laden. It would be complicit for us to refrain from action when drones are destroying the lives of innocent mothers and children. War is a very controversial, touchy subject that sparks great emotion and leads to division too often. As a person who's brother served in the Iraq War, I can relate firsthand to the constant fear and worry. It was a major burden of relief upon his return home.

For the millions of Americans who will not have the privilege of seeing their loved ones return home, the animosity for war is to be expected. No one favors sending their loved ones off to never see them again. We must make it clear that every obstacle does not call for the option of war; however, it must be on the table. While it must not be the very first option, war must be taken seriously when millions of American lives are at risk. In the midst of great fear and sacrifice, we must accept our long-term responsibilities for the future. We must defeat all of those who pose a threat to freedom and peace in America and throughout the world.

America's foreign policy was summed up best by these very words from President Reagan: "We are not going to betray our friends, reward the enemies of freedom, or permit fear and retreat to become American policies, especially in this hemisphere." During the toughest and dangerous of situations, America must never demonstrate weakness and shrink from the duties to prevent the loss of innocent lives. We must never appease to the demands of the enemy or negotiate with terrorists. America must always stand firm in its commitment to stability and peace. The world continues to look to this great nation for leadership, and we must never relent from our pursuit to deliver. Let us apologize never again for who we are as the world's most exceptional nation; let us embrace our history and who we are and must continue to be.

Defeating Evil in the 21st Century

We live in a very risky and dangerous world today. It is greatly different from the secure and stable world left behind by President Reagan after victory of the Cold War. The enemy we stand against today have deliberate intentions to obliterate and destroy the entire face of mankind. We must understand the depth and vitality of those who seek global dominance. Our enemy is composed of a radical faction of Islam. Centuries ago, a great deal of land was taken away from Muslims in the Middle-East. This land is very sacred to them and has deep significance. The jihadist radicals are responsible for re-acquiring the land taken in the past. They have intentions to conquer the lives of the citizens in those countries. The foundation they intend to impose is laid out in the Holy Koran. Radical Islamists in the Middle-East are hell-bent on conquering nearby countries and the millions of men, women, and children who reside in them. However, there is one obstacle committed to apprehending their acts of domination: The United States of America.

There is no way in Hell America will ever relent to the sidelines while a radical force of evil attempts to take over the world and impose its beliefs on as many people as it wishes. This is the fundamental motive behind the Radical Islamic attempt to destroy our wonderful country. They want the lives of every American brought to a state of non-existence. These people heavily despise America's free society based on the freedom and natural rights of the individual. Radical Islam seeks to destroy the state of Israel also. To be clear, not every single Muslim individual is a subscriber of the radical faction of Islam. There are many Muslims who advocate the respect and dignity of all human beings, as well as the spread of stability and peace. Because they reject the radical ideology, many Muslims have been subjected to persecution and death itself.

The very action we as Americans should refrain from is castigating all Muslims as evil and deserving of death. This would be nothing more than displaying acts of bigotry and willful ignorance. We must also do everything in our power to prevent Iran from obtaining a nuclear weapon. America must act with the same temperament and strength as we did to the Soviet empire. We must use the same resolve and force to defeat Radical Islamic-jihadist terrorism and leave it on the ash heap of history. America must commit to a world where all nuclear weapons are banished from the face of the Earth. Peace, liberty, and democracy must be our fundamental goals for the future.

Our Commitment to Humanity

America has been committed long to shaping a more perfect world for generations to come. We are by no means the cause of all of the ills that exist across the globe as some may proclaim. All of those who would make such a statement should check their homework. It is not shocking because they have been made for years. While it does make me very angry, I never lose faith and confidence in our ability to create a better world for everyone to live in. Our children deserve a world where they can sleep peacefully at night with hope for a greater tomorrow. The citizens in nations where there is no freedom and stability deserve the optimism of someday being in control of their own destiny. The people who have endured the suffering of disease and bondage of sexual captivity must receive the light of tomorrow. The United States must continue to shine as that one and only light the world looks to for a grander future.

"There is no arsenal or weapon in the arsenals of the world that is as formidable as the will and moral courage of free men and women. It is a weapon that our adversaries in today's world do not have; it is a weapon that we as Americans do have."

~President Ronald Reagan

Chapter 6

Abortion Is Murder

People ask me all the time for the reason I value life so much. It extends as far back to the days of my early childhood. My love for life never wavered in the midst of struggle and great challenge. I have desired to always live beyond the age of one hundred years old. Sometimes I would question my own reasoning even for loving life so very much. As I became older and grew a deep connection with God, life became far more important and admirable than before. Life can consist of either two things; it can consist of overcoming all challenges and rising to greatness or living in misery and despair with no plan to escape.

Life for me is about having a vision at heart with a plan to fulfill it in its entirety. In acknowledging that every person is a unique individual with many gifts from God, I am inspired long-term with faith that I can accomplish all of the dreams in my heart. Every person has the power of life in his or her very own hands to shape it best for the future. I take great peace in knowing that others' lives can become great because of my own. Life offers the opportunity to obtain whatever greatness and prosperity we desire. This will forever be the truth; in the midst of great crisis and uncertainty or stability and peace. I am grateful to have received these virtues to heart beginning at the age of sixteen. The greatest aspect of it all is the fact that every human being on Earth can experience the very same reality.

Life Begins at Conception

It was upon receiving Christ into my life when I began to learn the true uniqueness of life. I realized each and every person has a special gift from God to live a wonderful life. All of us have potential that is deep within our hearts to achieve greatness for the future. We are all blessed here on Earth to make a difference for a better world. God knows who we are before we are born even. Every individual born should be offered the best opportunities and nurtured as a child with the ability to prosper. It offends and angers me greatly in knowing that an actual person holds the power to store the virtue of life in jeopardy. I am disheartened to the core that an unborn child can have his or her life taken away without consent.

Life in the wound is only a very small beginning yet vital stage in completing the journey we are called to travel. It is the growth process of a human being in reaching the state of physical independence. During this stage, the child is attached to the mother by the umbilical cord, which makes them both one. When the mother decides to have an abortion procedure, she is not only ending the life of her unborn child, but she is killing a part of herself also. The unborn child's life is stripped away forever with no choice in the matter; he or she has the opportunity no longer to experience the world and fulfill his or her God-given calling.

No person should possess the right to end the life of another human being; it should not exist in the ability of anyone to suppress those who cannot speak and fend for themselves. A child growing inside his or her mother's wound has done absolutely nothing wrong to be punished with death. The child cannot resist or reverse the act of the abortion procedure being performed to kill him or her. The act of abortion is no different from death outside of the wound; it is the profound lack of respect for human life at one of its most essential stages. The power in any single human being on Earth reaches far beyond our imaginations. The person who was aborted just five seconds ago could have developed the cure for cancer, diabetes, and countless other deadly afflictions. The unborn child who will be aborted tomorrow could be the person to invent the next greatest form of technology that will shape humanity and bind it together. The child who is being aborted at this very moment could have the anointing to impact your life in a great manner. These are the powerful possibilities that are within in the power of life; no single person must possess the power to destroy them.

Protecting the Unborn

The path to preserve the gift of life for every child must be a fundamental priority in this country. I have stood passionately in the effort of doing so. It continues to sadden me to the core that thousands of unborn children are aborted each day. I realize there was the chance I could have been one of them. It becomes far more personal as I envision my children in future years. I am reminded of my obligation to ensure their safety and protection against those who would impose danger. I will never relent from the effort of protecting the profound sacredness of human life in America by seeking to end the practice of abortions in this country. The journey to reverse the practice of abortions will be the most difficult ever, but the result will be worth the price in the long-term. The millions of unborn children who could be saved will be grateful that we endured the long, agonizing battle to secure them.

The journey of protecting the unborn will be difficult due to the liberals on Capitol Hill who are pursuing a pro-abortion agenda. The Left continues to advocate federal funding for abortion through Planned Parenthood. While the House passed the Pain-Capable Unborn Child Act, authored by Congressman Franks of Arizona, the Democratic-controlled Senate opposed it unanimously. The President said himself he would veto the bill if it reached his desk. I was disappointed very highly after receiving knowledge of this. The bill would have banned the practice of abortions after twenty weeks. Scientists have proven that unborn babies are able to feel the pain during an abortion procedure after twenty weeks. The Pain-Capable Unborn Child Act was introduced in response to the actions of abortion administer, Kermit Gosnell. He was convicted of multiple accounts of first-degree murder, alongside one account of manslaughter.

I continue to ask myself to this day a very simple question: what kind of person in a clear state of conscience would inflict pain on a twenty-week old unborn baby with absolutely no remorse? I question the character of any man or woman who would either do it him- or herself or encourage it. I am very angry and heartbroken that America has a leadership that believes it is perfectly acceptable to inflict pain on twenty-week old babies, who are defenseless with no means to reverse the pain. Any normal person with character and integrity would feel the exact same way. I have great faith, however, we will gain a pro-life majority in the Senate in 2014 as well as a president in 2016 who will fight to uphold the gift of life by protecting the unborn.

We must restrict all federal funding of abortion procedures and defund Planned Parenthood, which is the single largest provider for abortions in the United States. We must ensure that girls under the age of eighteen have a parent's or guardian's permission to receive an abortion. Individuals should know the gender of the unborn child prior to aborting. Overall, we must seek the full repeal of Roe v. Wade, which has resulted in tens of millions of deaths of unborn children. The statistics of the number of abortions in the United States are as follows: over fifty-six million abortions have occurred between 1973 and 2011; with thirteen million of those unborn children being African-American. Over 1.06 million abortions occurred in 2011; 1.13 occurred in 2010; 1.16 million in 2009; and 1.21 million in 2008. Over 1.29 million abortions were performed in 2002; 1.31 million in 2000; and 1.36 in 1996. Two-thousand, eight-hundred ninety-nine abortions occur each day in our country; one-thousand, two-hundred twelve occur every minute; and one every thirty seconds. All of this is nothing more than a list of numbers to some, but it means very much more in reality. More abortions occur in the United States than any other western industrialized nation.

Abortions consist of the cause of more deaths in the United States than war, crime, and disease altogether. Can you imagine walking along fifty-six million dead bodies on an open field? Our country is far too great to allow the death of tens of millions of unborn children. This weighs heavily against the foundation which makes America the world's most exceptional society. Abortions violate the Declaration of Independence, which states, "We hold these truths to be self-evident that all men are created equal, that they are endowed by their Creator with certain 'unalienable rights', that among these are Life, Liberty, and the Pursuit of Happiness." Our government should be limited to a great extent, but it has a moral and sacred obligation to honor, protect, and preserve the life of every unborn child.

Sympathy for the Mother

It is critical we are reminded that not every single mother who has either aborted or considering to abort her unborn baby carries negative intentions. While there will always be those who will fail to assume responsibility for their actions, there will also be those who require assistance. One of the worst things we can do is ridicule and castigate an individual in a very difficult situation. The women who have received and/or considering to receive an abortion deserve assistance and encouragement from their families, doctors, churches, and communities. They deserve to be in everyone's prayers and circle of friendship. They need to understand that the embryos growing inside of them represent the creation of beautiful life and beyond, which is the reason they should not kill them.

We should not regard women in these situations with disrespect and belittlement, but instead stand by their side and offer heartfelt compassion; we do not have to end the life of an unborn child in the pursuit of assisting the mom. I believe, however, that abortion is unacceptable in approximately all circumstances. The cases of rape and incest should not serve as exceptions. While these are very deep and terrible instances for which require great assistance, the unborn child does not deserve to have his or her life stripped away from him. It is not the fault of the unborn child that his or her mom endured the painful experience for which had taken place. An unborn child who is born as the result of rape or incest is no different and bears no less significance than a child who is conceived otherwise. He or she should be regarded with the very same dignity and respect. The fact remains that he or she has a wonderful gift from God and should experience all that life has to offer. The only case in which an abortion should be acceptable is to protect the life of the mother. I respect each and every one of those feel strongly that rape and incest are acceptable instances. It is far more important to store greater emphasis on the goal of preserving the life of the unborn in this great country.

Deception in Play

The Left continues to manipulate the American people time and time again. Those on the Left feels it is best to inflict division and warfare in every key issue there is. They have proclaimed the Republican Party as well as conservatives have engaged in a war on women in this country. The Left continues to claim Republicans are out of touch with women and their personal needs. This is only an attempt to distract us from the reality of the issue at hand, which is protecting the right of each and every person to experience life. The Left has declared war on not only the unborn, but the very foundation that which America was established upon in 1776. Liberal Democrats in Washington are fighting tooth-and-nail to dismantle the unique gift of life by every means of their disposal.

They refused to support the Pain-Capable Unborn Child Act, they continue to spend billions of taxpayer funds on abortion through Planned Parenthood, and they persist with the victimization of women and their health. It was President Clinton who vetoed the Partial-Birth Abortion Ban Act of 1995. Then-Senator Obama himself proclaimed that a baby who survives a late-term abortion procedure is "punishment." In the Illinois state senate, he voted no on a bill that would have banned the practices of live birth abortion. This is nothing more than an act of tyrannical genocide.

It angers me to the core of the extreme that all of this deliberate wrong is taking place. It is such a great moral calamity that unborn babies are being killed each and every day by encouragement of our very own government. While the President and fellows liberals on Capitol Hill believes the unborn is punishment, I believe all children are a unique gift from God as well as a blessing to the Earth and all of humanity. Our country depends on the unborn to secure the greatness of our founding. We need all of the talent and skills of the many potential teachers, doctors, entrepreneurs, and leaders to shape our future. Our overall goal must be to encourage the existence of the unborn and not exploit the American people. We must work to strengthen all of those mothers who have yet to become the greatest parents to their children possible.

Because the Left does not believe in people, it does not feel the need to speak the reality of the challenges before us and unite the nation around that purpose. The Left chooses to use abortion as a tool to divide the American people to advance its political agenda rather than stand for what is in the best interests of character. Those on the Left will continue to politicize the issue of life and every other for political expediency, even if it put the lives and well-being of the American people at stake. There is no war on women in America, by any means. There is a war, however, on the most sacred and wonderful gift from God to humanity: life.

My message to the President and the Left is very simple: no unborn child deserves to have his or her bones crushed or limbs or bodily organs smashed; no unborn child deserves to die at no fault of his or her own, but to enter the world and be held by his or her mom and dad. He or she deserves to grow up as a small child, play with toys, and watch Spongebob. Every unborn child deserves the chance to go to school, achieve the fullness of his or her potential, and become a doctor or lawyer or teacher or a future leader of this great country. They will have that chance because the day will come when Roe v. Wade is overturned and the gift of life has been preserved for every human being to come. Mr. President and the Left, the lives and dreams of the unborn belong not to any of you but to those of whom they were given, which extends none of you the right to take them away.

What if it Were You?

The issue of abortion is one of the most heart-touching and controversial of our time. It sparks deep passion and has very deep perspectives on both sides of the political spectrum. There are many well-intended aspirations from the many Americans who are advocates for the unborn as well as some of those who claim to be pro-choice. There is a great cry out for togetherness to protect life for the unborn. Our politics makes it beyond difficult for us to take the very best course of action to protect life. I would ask that you sit aside party and label and perspective and come out of the entire debate for just a moment.

Ask yourself a very important question: what if you were in a position where your life was at the precipice and there was absolutely nothing you could do to reverse it? What would you do? How would you feel or react? This would be an extremely difficult situation to be in, but it happens each and every day. It happens to millions of unborn babies throughout the world each day. The reality is harsh but simple; you would have never lived to meet your mother and father and the many others who love and care about you unconditionally and vice-versa. Those you may have impacted and touched would have never had the privilege of your presence during the times they needed you most.

Every moment of your life has made a difference in some way or another. You are the one in control of your life and should have full control over whether you will live or die. Even if your life turned out to be not so fortunate, no other should have the power to end it on their own behalf. What if your mom or dad or sibling or best friend was aborted? If this was the case, you would have never experienced the gift of life in the beginning, or your life would be very much different than it is today. This is not an issue such as homosexuality that is personal and affects no other in a negative manner. This is far beyond than just claiming a woman should maintain control over her own body because she is not the only person being affected by her decision. If your mother would have aborted you, you would not be here. Because your mother chose to not abort you, you are able to breathe, sleep, and wake up every single morning.

You were an unborn child just all of those who have been aborted. You were connected to your mother's body, which made the both of you one. However, you had your own body also. When you were inside your mother's wound, you belonged to both hers and your own body. There was blood pumping in and out of your heart just as a person living out of the wound. Stand grateful that you were not one of the fifty-six million unborn children who was aborted. Be grateful that you have received the gift of life with the opportunity to grow and prosper beyond the stars. I will pray and sacrifice for the millions of unborn children who will come today and tomorrow so they will be able to say "I love you, mom; I love you, dad. I love you, honey; I love you, my beautiful children and grandchildren."

"Once you bring life into the world, you must protect it. We must protect it by changing the world."

~Elie Wiesel

Chapter 7

Liberty and Justice for All

None of us in the United States of America will ever forget the long and very long, brutal-fought battle of the civil rights movement. This is an era for which defined the strength of our great nation like no other truly. It was a time when individuals of a certain kind were regarded as second-class citizens. All persons of color were regarded as inferior to all others. Some were beaten, violated in a sexual manner, and murdered even. We have heard and read of the many heart-wrenching accounts of those who endured the terrible scourges of discrimination, intolerance, and hate. Most of us in our generation will never be able to relate to the pain felt by our ancestors who came before. It took the selfless courage and character of heroes such as Rosa Parks and Dr. Martin Luther King, Jr. to stand and speak for those who could not do so by their own might. The path to freedom and equal treatment for all was the most difficult of tasks, but it was sought and achieved through perseverance as well as faith in the God who loves us all the same.

As a child, I did not understand the reality behind the goal of civil rights for every American citizen. It was through learning the truth of myself as a human being and the vision of our beloved Founders that I began to understand the civil rights movement. I learned it was far more than just equal treatment under the law. This was a key factor, however, as the discriminatory policies of the times were both unconstitutional and unjust. The underlying goal of civil rights was to establish the respect and dignity of individuals of every race. Leaders such as Dr. Martin Luther King, Jr. and Rosa Parks knew there would require more than just mere legislation to achieve togetherness.

The motives behind the discriminatory practices stood on pride and hate. Pride and hate are what sparked the water hoses and police brutality and beatings for which had taken place. This was the exact case for the segregationist policies that divided blacks and whites. There was the belief among some that they were superior to all others due to the color of their skin. As a result, those who were deemed as less important were denied recognition of their God-given rights. The greatest weapon capable of driving out hate and achieving full equal status for all of God's children was love. Civil rights would have meant nothing without a sense of respect and admiration for others at heart regardless of skin color.

There remains a great number of people who hold animosity and hate for persons from certain walks of life. Many of these people feel as if their kinds are superior to others. While we have come so far as a nation, we still have far to travel. The new civil rights struggle of our time is achieving full equal treatment for individuals in America of every sexuality. The last thing we in America should do is carry on in the Twenty-first Century the same discriminatory and intolerant practices that shook our foundation in the past.

Freedom Belongs to All

One of the principles that makes America exceptional to every corner of the world is our belief that each individual should be free and in control of his or her own destiny. This ideal continues to reward millions of Americans and people abroad with a prosperity far beyond the average imagination. The founders of our great country ensured this God-given privilege for not only some, but everyone. Each and every single one of us are bestowed with the God-given 'unalienable rights' of Life, Liberty, and the Pursuit of Happiness. No government or fellow institutions of Man can take them away under any circumstances. The primary objective of the civil rights movement during the 1950s and 60s was to reaffirm our Founders' vision once again; a fellow objective was to ensure the protection of these rights for all Americans, not just some.

It is clearly unconstitutional to prohibit gays and lesbians from sharing in certain privileges as heterosexuals. To deny marriage, civil unions, federal benefits, hospital visits, customer service, and military service to an individual on the basis of sexual orientation extends far beyond the underlying principles upon which America was established. An individual has every right to believe marriage is between a man and woman only, but he or she should not have the right to force this belief on those who have chosen a separate path. This premise follows with civil unions the same. Federal benefits are financed by taxpayer dollars from Americans of all kinds, which means they cannot be denied to a group of people on the basis of race, gender, sexual orientation, etc. Every American who loves his or her country should be able to defend it in battle. It stands against everything upon which our nation was established to regard individuals in the LGBT community or any other as inferior in contrast to everyone else. Absolutely nowhere does it state in the Declaration of Independence or the Constitution that gays and lesbians can or must denied certain rights and privileges.

I will disagree forever with those who believe ensuring natural rights for individuals in the LGBT community differs from the civil rights struggle. One of the principal reasons people of color were regarded with such great belittlement was that some believed themselves and their way of life to be superior to others. There are people who feel as if their customs and beliefs matter more than those who believe differently. Many of them feel the LGBT community poses a threat to our country. Very much to the contrary, it is this sense of intolerance and bigotry on the part of some that poses a fundamental threat to everything we stand for in the United States of America. I would like to make it very clear that it is not intolerant to believe in something strongly to the point where you will defend it with your life; it becomes intolerance once it leads to the point of forcing it by either law or constant ridicule and persecution on those who believe and behave differently.

It does not pose a threat for everyone to be treated as equal. All who are gay, lesbian, bisexual, and transgender deserve to carry out their lives just as much as the rest of us. If some are concerned about homosexuality on television and the media, I would remind them that a person can pick up the remote and change the channel easily. Parents can monitor what their children view on television through a code system on their cable system. This limits the type of channels and programs that can be viewed.

Why must society pick on homosexuality? In this great country in which we have been blessed to live, we should accept one another for who we are and realize we are all one. We stand as one nation, and we are all Americans. We will never live up to our founders' vision fully until we abolish all laws and forms of discrimination towards the LGBT community as well as others. We must repeal the Defense of Marriage Act, ensure same-sex couples the same benefits as heterosexual couples enjoy, and continue to scale back the scourge of hate crimes and unethical treatment of those who are gay, lesbian, bisexual, and transgender. Freedom is a natural right that belongs every man and woman; it is not a special privilege for a selected few. Everyone should have the freedom to live his or her life not only by law, but with assurance and peace at heart. The time that individuals in the LGBT community are regarded as inferior in America must end. There is no one among us who is of more or less worth than any other; for we are all the children of God, and everyone in this country should be regarded with the same respect and dignity in the eyes of the law as American citizens.

A government that continues to spend our nation trillions of dollars into debt, purchases oil from countries that loath us, fails to strengthen the foundation for economic certainty, and falls short to provide for those who have served our country with the greatest honor should not dictate to the American people how they can and cannot lead their personal lives. Government should choose destiny for no single individual in this country. This may be the reality in places such as Russia, China, and the Middle East, but not here in the United States of America, the freest, greatest, and most prosperous society in all of the history of human civilization.

Love Thy Neighbor as Thy Self

One of the most important things in my life has always been my Christian faith. It provides my heart with a foundation of peace, stability, and optimism for the future. It has brought my life to a great new level over the years, and I am never ashamed to make it known to others. From my perspective, a Christian has a fundamental objective to be Christ-like. The greatest gift from Jesus Christ to the world during His time was love. Everything He stood for revolved around the principle that we should love our sisters and brothers as we would want them to love us. Christ believed we should stand by each other and lift one another. He taught us to forgive and pray for those who do evil to us.

Christ taught that we should do onto others in the same manner we would prefer to be done unto us. One of the greatest things we were taught by our Lord and Savior was to not judge and condemn. All of these are many ways Christ has called us to love. In loving others, we love Christ. When these principles of Christ are met with obedience, we are brought closer together and able to overcome challenges with great significance. My personal relationship with Jesus Christ has given me the ability to perform the duties He commanded better over time. His principles of love define my approach to individuals of every kind, including those who are homosexual, lesbian, bisexual, and transgender. Christ died for those in the LGBT community as the rest of us; they are children of God as we all are.

I am angered when many fellow Christians attempt to elevate the sin of homosexuality to a pedestal as if it is the most dangerous sin there is. Much of the reasoning behind this is to justify their own sin and iniquities. They feel as if they are doing a favor to the will of God by regarding gays and lesbians with less value. They feel that forcing their view of the world on those who have chosen the opposite path is the best way to lead others to Christ. This cannot be further from the love of Christ than it is currently. If someone chooses to live contrary to biblical principles, our objectives in accordance to Christ are to stand by the person's side and lead by example in Christ-like character. We are not to judge or chastise the person through condemnation. Our place is not to dictate to anyone how to live and discriminate against him or her if he or she decides ultimately to live differently.

To prohibit marriage, civil unions, customer service, and/or federal benefits on the basis of sexual orientation is judgment and condemnation and goes against everything Christ taught us. Those who feel they are doing a favor to Christ are in for a rude awakening. It states in James 2:10-11, "For whoever keeps the whole law but fails in one point has become accountable for all of it. For He who said, 'Do not commit adultery,' also said, 'Do not commit murder.' If you do not commit adultery but do commit murder, you have become a transgressor of the law." It states in Romans 3:23, "For all have sinned and fallen short of the glory of God." These verses support the fact that all sin is equal, so makes it no sense and does no good to elevate homosexuality or any other iniquity to a higher pedestal.

It does no favor to anyone to infringe upon someone's personal life and constitutional protections. In fact, it causes pain and heartbreak to those who are gay and lesbian and pushes everyone further away from one another. As a result, we will encounter greater difficulty in solving challenges that affects all of God's children as a whole such as poverty, crime, joblessness, and the threat of terrorism. It becomes more difficult to instill in our children the true character Christ. We as Americans should not view or treat an individual differently on the basis of their sexuality. Someone who is gay, lesbian, bisexual, or transgender is no different or more or less better in the eyes of God than someone who is heterosexual. An individual part of the LGBT community is no more guilty of sin than someone who fornicates, adulterates, steals, murders, or swears. Furthermore, someone who happens to be gay or lesbian is not affecting anyone in a negative manner by living his or her lifestyle. Homosexuality should not define a person's entire character, just as someone who swears or fornicates or steals. Each of us hold different motivations behind certain decisions, which is one of the reasons Christ taught us to not judge and condemn.

There has always been the question of whether an individual is born into the world as a homosexual, lesbian, or bisexual or if he or she chooses to be that way. My perspective on the matter is simple. First: each of us were born as a sinner, and, as proclaimed previously, homosexuality is a sin just as any other. Secondly and final: should it matter? When will we begin to build a world where every person can wake up and walk in acceptance without judgment and castigation? When will we stop trying to be judges of men and become Disciples of Christ? The job of judge is taken by God Himself already belongs to absolutely no other.

Every one of us holds a spot in both Heaven and Hell and is responsible for choosing which spot to take. No matter how much sin we have committed in the eyes of God, we have an opportunity for redemption and salvation through our Lord and Savior, Jesus Christ. It is time we begin to love one another as Christ loves us all. We must stand by one another and lead others in the way Christ would. Our Lord does not see color, gender, or sexual preference; He sees the heart. We will never live up to the true, abundant love of Christ until we see the same.

Standing for Freedom and Equal Treatment

It is time the Republican Party itself declares its overall support for full equal treatment for the LGBT community in the eyes of the law. As stated in the first chapter, the Republican Party was founded to reaffirm the principle that all should be masters of their own destinies. This principle carries forward to this very day. It was the Republican Party that abolished the separate and unequal treatment of African-Americans during the 1860s and set the stage for civil rights and equality under law. To continue to stand opposed to gay rights and marriage equality would be not only a serious mistake, but a major contradiction to the party's history and its core, underlying ideal of personal sovereignty.

The party cannot continue to alienate Americans of a certain kind and lump them into an inferior group or class; this is what separates Republicans from Democrats. The Democratic Party separates Americans into members of groups, but the Republican Party recognizes all the people of America as individuals. I am Republican because I believe all persons are unique human beings with both a heart and gift of God; also because I believe strongly in liberty, equality, and opportunity. It is important that the party is consistent with these principles in its overall vision in keeping our nation the strong and proud land it is and must remain.

Each and every person in this country is guaranteed the freedom by the Declaration of Independence and the Constitution to live as he or she wishes as long as he or she is not harming others. We must stand very strongly for this sacred promise without waver or compromise. Generations long before us have sacrificed and fought too long for us to relent on what makes America what she is. The journey towards protecting the Life, Liberty, and Pursuit of Happiness of gays and lesbians all across America is the new civil rights struggle of our time. It is about standing up for the dignity and respect of all men and women. We must never again throughout the course of history treat any person or persons differently because they do not agree with our personal standards or fit our methods of doing things. The great news is that the natural rights are beginning to be recognized for same-sex couples in many states across the nation. We must continue the fight to recognize the rights of all here at home. As the leader of the free world, it is critical that all of America's citizens are free themselves. We must also speak out against the stoning and mistreatment of homosexuals on the continent of Africa and other places.

I disagree respectfully with those who are not in favor with the movement for equal rights and treatment for the LGBT community. While some do so on the sole basis of intolerance, many of them are good-hearted individuals with the soundest of intentions. However, they still cannot and should not have the right to judge and dictate the course of life of any other just because they feel their way of life is more appropriate and acceptable. This may work in the Middle East or Russia or China, but not here in the United States of America. We are a representative democracy and will be always. Tolerance is not accepting the ways of others; it is accepting others even when they do not share your own. It does not require that someone must agree with everything others do; it also does not mean that someone has the right to discriminate against others. The only thing we in America should be intolerant of is intolerance itself.

"Tolerance implies no lack of commitment to one's own beliefs. Rather it condemns the oppression or persecution of others."

~President John F. Kennedy

Chapter 8

Restoring Morality and the Family

One of the things I will be forever grateful for is the foundation of values that defines my life. I hold the values of hard work, self-respect, determination, and perseverance to be very sacred. I take heart also to integrity, self-discipline, and respect for others. The value I take to heart the most is strong character, which defines every aspect of someone's life. The greater the character of someone, the greater life path he or she will choose. I feel as if I am a greater person in the eyes of God and humanity for the character I choose to adhere to. As I am very grateful for God's help in becoming who I am, I am grateful also very highly for my parents who raised me from childhood to adulthood. They instilled in me the desire of achieving an education to avoid financial struggles in the future and become all I can be.

My parents encouraged me to avoid the use of alcohol (until the age of 21 with moderation) and drug use, as well as association with negative crowds of people. As a child growing up, my mom kept me at home to a great extent, even during part of my teenage years. My parents spent a great deal of time with me as I was a child growing up. All of this played a significant role in making me the man I am today; it was a very strong bond to parents who cares very much and the values I learned as a result. Because I was taught the difference between right and wrong, my life will prosper in the long-term.

Our nation was established upon the values of individual liberty, personal freedom, and national stability. All of us value the promises of living in a free society because it allows us to be happy and stable in our own ways. However, the Founders of our country had something far greater in store to pass on. They issued a challenge to future generations to uphold a profound sense of moral consciousness. They desired for society to stand upon a strong, steady foundation where individuals would practice what they know deeply in their hearts is right and morally sound. I believe very strongly in a vision where people honored and respected the things that bring greatness, hope, and opportunity. The strength of American culture has always been predicated upon strong families and churches, which leads to socially productive neighborhoods and communities. When people in their individual communities take pride in virtues that are important to life and progress, they are able to lead lives of successful achievement, sufficiency, and long-term prosperity. Much that is taking place in our culture today, however, is totally anathema to this vision.

The Foundation of Morality and the American Family

Many important issues such as economic growth, education reform, fiscal stability, and world peace have been discussed throughout this book. Each one of these that has been discussed so far is highly critical in securing our nation's future. Every American deserves a shot at the American Dream, safety from harm abroad, and to have their constitutional privileges protected. To perfect America to the core truly, we must explore the underlying ideal for which has defined our great country for centuries.

Throughout history, there has always existed both the rise and fall of civilizations. Many of the greatest empires such as the Ottoman, Persian, and Roman have seen their magnificent beginnings and tragic downfalls. History has proven very well that many things come to an end. All of us should ask ourselves why so many of the greatest societies of the world realized their fate. As many of them were established, they were built upon their visions of an exceptional foundation with a set of core principles to be adhered to. The principles and values that which the original foundation was based were always intended to be passed down from generation to generation. A society's framers understood deeply that in order for their society to remain and continue to grow, future generations of individuals must live by the ideals upon which the society was established. As the citizens began to drift away from certain fundamental beliefs and customs, they would become something that is totally anathema to the vision of their original vision. This is exactly what is happening in the United States of America.

History has taught us that our nation's future depends on our children heavily. A child will lead either a productive or counterproductive life depending very strongly on his or her upbringing. An individual will adhere to a lifestyle based on either strong character and unleashing the potential that is within or negative behavior that inflicts harm on him- or herself and others. The difference depends upon how someone is raised from childhood to adulthood. When a child is very young, he or she has very little knowledge of right from wrong. Children tend to duplicate the actions of those around them, just as anyone who knows no better in particular situations. If a child is exposed to swearing, violence, and promiscuity, he or she is very likely to adapt much of the same behavior during the years leading up to adolescent hood and adulthood eventually. A child who is exposed to drug and/or alcohol use is very likely to become addicted to one of the following or both as he or she becomes an adult. To the contrary, a child who is taught that all of these activities are very counterproductive is more than likely to refrain from them later on.

Children who are raised on a foundation of character, self-discipline, and personal integrity are very much likely to make positive decisions as they become older. No person is born with a certain value system automatically; it is instilled by the mother and father. An alcoholic, drug user, fornicator, criminal, or even a racist does not become this way without some outside influence. There is very much of this taking place throughout America, which has led to the breakdown of many of our neighborhoods and communities. The question before us is very simple: what has led to the breakdown of moral principles and values?

Contrary to a vision where children are working diligently in school, believing in themselves, and exemplifying positive character, many adolescents are plagued by drug abuse, gang violence, alcoholism, and under age sexual activity. Many of them are dropping out of school and abandoning their career aspirations also. Our children are growing up in a culture where they are taught to be morally relative rather than morally conscious. The liberal media and pop culture have taken the liberty of defining the behavior that individuals should adapt to. If someone does not adapt to a certain belief system or set of principles, he or she will encounter persecution and humiliation. Young people today are living in a society where they are pressured to practice behaviors that others practice; all in the name of popularity and acceptance.

This is incredibly dangerous for not only our generation, but for those to come in future years. All of those who have come before us worked their hearts out to pass on a better life onto their children (us). They raised their offspring to be productive contributors to society and to not be disgraceful, unproductive individuals. When people are young and do not know any better, they have a fear of being criticized and castigated by the world. If you were to view the much broader scale of the situation, you would realize the future is so much more important. When teenagers have sex, drink alcohol, and consume drugs, they are so much more likely to encounter poverty, prison, and death.

Many adolescents see very little wrong with consuming alcohol and drugs, engaging in sexual recklessness, and taking education not as seriously as they should. While they are enjoying the short-term benefits of these decisions, they fail to see the long-term destruction that lies ahead. Some are not affected emotionally even by the deadly consequences of them, either. When people educate some adolescents on the destruction that can result from certain behavior choices, some of them regard their helpers as the ones who are wrong. I would describe the situation as viewing them from afar in a crystal ball and observing everything that is happening. The moral crisis we face in America is due to a lack of strong, adequate values being taught to individuals by their parents as they are growing up. No matter what may be proclaimed or what statistics may state, our society is deeply embedded in a crisis of culture, and, if we do not reverse course immediately, we will reach the point where it will be so much more difficult to make our country morally strong again.

A foundation of moral consciousness and positive character in America begins very heavily with the vitality and strength of the family. The family structure plays a major role in shaping our country to what it must be. A family is not required to be very large in size; it can consist of just two parents and one child. The beginning of every family structure begins with God, whose providence blesses the overall stability of everyone. With God at the very top, the structure branches off into the mother and father. With the mother at left and father at right, the structure branches off into the child. There is God at the top with the mother and father at left and right below, with the child at the center below. I stand opposed very adamantly and diligently to any and all forces that pose a threat to the overall vitality and strength of the American family.

Teenage sexual activity, which results in unwanted prenancies, poses the greatest threat to the family structure in this country. Someone in his or her teenage years are not equipped yet fully with the resources and tools required to pursue a productive lifestyle, which means there is very little to pass onto a child. An individual in his or her teenage years is in the process still of obtaining the best education and determining possible life paths to pursue. How is it possible for someone who does not possess the fundamental virtues of life to care for a child successfully and adequately? How can a teenager pass on the importance of getting an education and the process of strong decision-making if he or she has not been instilled with them? In simpler terms, how can a child raise a child?! The only result that is likely to take place is the child growing up without the proper life skills and training that is required to master his or her destiny, and this is what has been taking place for generations, particularly in minority communities. The child is also likely to grow up without the presence of a father, which would result most likely in greater poverty and the increasing possibilities of drug and alcohol use and crime while growing up.

I was raised by a mother and father who were well capable and old enough to raise children. This is the reason they were able to instill in me all of the things for me to become the person I am today. I would not be who I am today if they would have conceived me at a very young age or if my father was not present in my life. The human brain does not develop fully until the age of twenty-five, which proves that teenagers are still growing themselves, furthermore. The most proper scenario for extending birth to a child is a married couple where both partners have pursued successful careers and are well into their late twenties or early thirties. When married, committed couples of age with successful careers give birth to children, the odds for poverty and indecency decrease heavily. A child is also more likely to respect someone who is older, more successful, and greater experienced than someone who is still in the process of being raised him- or herself. While mistakes will happen regardless, the very last thing we as a society should encourage is teenage child birth; for this will only endanger the child and society as a whole as time proceeds.

Reaching the Pendulum

No matter what the situation may consist of, there is always the possibility of being too late. There has been those already to deem our society as being too deep in crisis to be saved. As we view our present situation, it is very understandable for one to develop such a conclusion. When we continue to witness more and more young adults having children, obtaining diseases, going to prison, dying of alcoholism, and dropping out of school with no hope, it is expected for some to become discouraged and disillusioned. However, I believe firmly that we have both an opportunity and the ability to re-examine ourselves not only as individuals, but as a people. We have the chance to reclaim the lost virtues that have made us great in past. We also have a solemn obligation to teach young people what it means to love God truly and store Him at the center of their lives; for He is critical in restoring and maintaining moral stability in our society.

Resolving our moral crisis will lie in our homes, schools, and churches in every individual community in America. It is the responsibility of parents to instill in their sons and daughters the profound importance in getting the best education, and teaching them how to be civilized, morally conscious individuals. Our children must be taught the destructiveness in alcoholism, drug use, gun violence, and sexual irresponsibility. Schools have the responsibility of holding students highly accountable and offering advice and counseling on moral character and strong, adequate judgment. Churches have the obligation to confront the issues in their communities such as mending the lives being devastated and destroyed by drug and alcohol use and deadly sexual diseases and assisting individuals in discovering their divine gifts. Society as a whole must teach young people how to believe in themselves, demonstrate self-confidence, and fulfill their God-given potential. There must also be incentives for children as they adhere to sound character; for what gets rewarded gets repeated. All of these initiatives will help us revive from moral crisis and pass on a stronger, better society onto our generations to come.

There are some who believe that moral character can forced down by the hands of government. Some believe the moral breakdown in our country calls for more laws and greater government involvement in our personal lives. The aspect that is most ironic is that many of these voices are not those of liberals but conservatives! Values can be handed down by parents only; if a child is not taught right from wrong by his or her parents and how to be a productive individual, then there is very little government can do. Government also should not continue to subsidize the family breakdown by advancing the incentives of the welfare state, penalizing marriage with less benefits, and increasing incentives to have children out of wedlock.

There remains a great number of individuals who are afflicted by both drug and alcohol use; there remains many who are sexually irresponsible also. Crime rates continue to increase dramatically. While those who harm the lives and well-being of others should be held accountable by law, it should not end here. Infringing upon the Second Amendment will not solve the issue of crime; limiting access to birth control, more anti-drug enforcement laws, and prohibition will not overcome the reality of our challenges. The only outcome that will occur as a result of more restriction is greater rebellion. Laws cannot solve the void in the hearts of those who have been taught no better. Because some know no greater behavior, they will be forced emotionally and automatically to rebel. Government subsidizes the problem only; just as it cannot end poverty, it cannot end immorality. It cannot raise a child as well or efficiently as his or her mother and father. If someone is taught right from wrong as a child, he or she will either do something or not because in the heart he or she knows it is for the best. The individual will know what is best based on what has been instilled in the heart from birth to adulthood.

I will never forget four years ago when I attended a going-away party for a friend who was headed to Germany for one year for a student foreign exchange program. During this time, I was sixteen years old only. I was unaware there was going to be great amounts of alcohol present. I was the only person in my age group who did not drink alcohol. While I was tempted to a fair degree to do so, I did not consume any alcohol because of what I was taught as a child. It was not because of the age restriction of twenty-one so much, but I was reminded of what my parents instilled in me. When I recall that time, I am very grateful for my parents who taught me how to stand on principle and what principles to stand on. More laws and constant nagging are not the answer; for the exception of people who harm others, which requires law enforcement, the best solutions to help those who have chosen a negative path but are not affecting others in a negative manner are prayer and guidance from family, friends, and society.

America will never arise from the depths of moral crisis until the family is restored. If we do not revive the family in this country, we will continue to falter, morally and socially. When the family declines, so does society. When society crumbles, so does the country. When America falters, so goes the world. I believe with all of my heart that we as a country can rise above the state of moral crisis. I believe in our power to overcome every major ill of society and send each of them back to where they originated from. By all means shall the foundation of morality and the American family be restored to full vitality and strength so we offer our children the future they so deserve.

"Train up a child in the way he should go; and when he is old he will not depart from it."

~Proverbs 22:6

Epilogue

It is beyond critical that our children inherit an America filled with the hope to fulfill their greatest dreams and highest aspirations. They deserve to live in a nation where they are free and in control of their very own lives and destinies. All of us in the current generation have a moral obligation to bestow onto them the future they so deserve. We have an obligation to return America to its founding ideals of limited government, personal sovereignty, and morality; we must pass onto our children an economy that provides ladders of opportunity for every child, an education system that will answer the call of their hearts' desires, a society where they are regarded as individual human beings with the ability to think and do for themselves, a society with strong families and communities where values are vibrant, and a world at stability and peace.

What shall history bear witness to when subsequent generations recall our resolve in restoring our nation's overall strength? Will we answer the call of fate and pursue the difficult and unpopular course that stands before us? Or will we ignore the sacrifices made by our Founding Fathers and generations before us? Every obstacle we face can be overcame; for it is our obstacles for which defines America's resolve and makes us stronger than before. There was never a time when we have shrunken from the demands of time. We have risen to the demands of every generation; we stood in allegiance to the things and ideas that have defined us for over two centuries, and, as a result, we have risen to greatness. America has remained the greatest, most exceptional society ever known by human civilization. Let us cease never in living up to the American spirit, which has carried us throughout the course of history; let us fail never to keep the promises made by our ancestors; let us stand firm with faith in our very own Creator.

It is each and every one of us; the mothers and fathers; students and teachers; entrepreneurs and small business owners; schools and churches; and neighborhoods and communities who will determine our future. Parents must teach their children to believe in themselves and demonstrate positive character. Businesses must create the jobs of tomorrow that will extend opportunity to citizens everywhere. Students must demonstrate a willingness to succeed and teachers must teach them the skills they need. Schools and churches must create a positive environment for our young people and hold them accountable. Neighborhoods and communities must come together and do what must be done to improve the lives of their people; there must be great emphasis on the growth of education, entrepreneurialism, and lawful citizenship. All of these things have the potential of not only eradicating poverty, but shining a new light of hope and optimism upon those in the dark.

Government should do those things which are authorized by the Constitution only; all other duties are to be reserved to the states or to the people. Government cannot create jobs or educate our children or legislate morality; only the free market and private citizens can do these things most efficiently. The people know better to conduct their everyday lives than a group of bureaucrats thousands of miles away whom have never been met or seen. When government attempts to do what was unintended, things go wrong; the freedom of individuals are threatened, as well as our nation's overall stability. We have seen this in the form of Obamacare; it has not and will not solve the underlying problems in our healthcare system, which are the rising costs of care and unaffordability. Many people advocate for greater government involvement in the name of compassion. Compassion is possessing the willingness to lift and help others. Someone who would hurt and destroy others for the sole purpose of power does not possess compassion. Real compassion is not giving a man fish and feeding him for a day only; it is teaching a man to fish to feed him for the remainder of his natural life. Compassion is upliftment; entitlement is complicity. The best form of compassion that exists is helping an individual to acquire the ability to do for self rather than government do for him or her.

The liberal establishment, which consists of the majority of the Democratic Party, cares for nothing more than power and control. The Left will perform whatever action necessary in pursuit of power. It portrays itself as advocates for families and communities and to stand for tolerance and assist those in America who need it most; however, liberals are the total opposite of these things. Instead of recognizing the uniqueness of every American, liberals would rather divide us in regards to what we look like or how much money we make. They would rather an individual be dependent on the government rather than possess the tools to be responsible for him- or herself. Those on the Left will persecute and demonize anyone who disagrees with their world view and does not fit their standards. While they depend on the ignorance of some, liberals seek to control the nation through political correctness and government dependency. The Left knows as long as America is divided among herself and totally dependent upon government that it will remain in power.

We as the American people cannot sit back and let this continue to take place before our very eyes. To some of us who lead our lives with bitterness and little hope as we say to ourselves and others that this is the way it will always be and there is nothing or no one who can change it, we must realize that it is this very attitude that allows for our situation to become no better. As the American people, we must realize that this country belongs to each and every one of us and that our children are depending on us to stand for them. Let us feed power into the fangs of the liberal establishment any longer; let us transform our frustrations, bitterness, and pessimism into the energy and drive that will take our nation back.

I have great faith for our nation's future; not only will we overcome, but hope will be restored to the hearts of millions all across America. Our children will inherit a world greater than the one we live in today. They will wake up each and every morning with the drive and desire to conquer their dreams and achieve their hearts' desires. Subsequent generations will recall history with great pride and admiration. We will not only prosper as we did during the 1980s, but far greater. The prosperity will last and extend to generations to come after. There is no end for America; for her sunrise will shine forever and ever. The dawn of America's greatness shall forever live on, and, in the words of President Reagan, "why shouldn't we believe that? We are Americans."

"We have it in our power to begin the world over again."

~Thomas Paine

www.ingramcontent.com/pod-product-compliance
Lightning Source LLC
Chambersburg PA
CBHW060407290526
45791CB00002B/650